TEA & CAKE

WITH

LISA FAULKNER

TEA & CAKE

WITH

LISA FAULKNER

**SIMON &
SCHUSTER**

London · New York · Sydney · Toronto · New Delhi

A CBS COMPANY

First published in Great Britain in 2015
by Simon & Schuster UK Ltd
A CBS Company

Text Copyright © Lisa Faulkner 2015
Design Copyright © Simon & Schuster UK 2015

10 9 8 7 6 5 4 3 2 1

Simon & Schuster UK Ltd
222 Gray's Inn Road
London
WC1X 8HB

www.simonandschuster.co.uk

Simon & Schuster Australia, Sydney
Simon & Schuster India, New Delhi

A CIP catalogue record for this book is available
from the British Library

ISBN 978-1-47112-560-7

Project Editor: Laura Herring
Designer: Two Associates
Photographer: Chris Terry (small images, Lisa's own)
Home Economists: Richard Harris and Lizzie Kamenetzky
Stylists: Polly Webb-Wilson and Olivia Wardle
Hair and Make-up: Justine Wade
Production Manager: Katherine Thornton
Make-up: with thanks to Kiehls, Lancôme, Liz Earle and Smashbox
Colour reproduction by Aylesbury Studios Ltd, UK
Printed and bound in Italy

*This book is dedicated to my wonderful
Nanna who showed us the true meaning of
unconditional love.*

1914 - 2014

CONTENTS

✳

WHY I BAKE

It's funny to say it, but I didn't used to consider myself a baker – I still don't, really! I make cakes and biscuits and little pies several times a week, but it's really so I have something to eat with a cup of tea. The biscuit tin is always full, ready for anybody to drop in, or just for me mid-afternoon! My mum and both grandmothers were the same, so baking, for me at least, makes me feel like I'm home. And that feeling is something I want to pass on to my daughter and to share with all those around me. You don't need to worry about everything turning out perfectly – it's not about making the lightest pastry or the crumbliest scone. What it's really about is taking the time to make something for someone – the simple gesture of pouring out a cup of tea and placing a plate of homemade biscuits alongside can make them feel loved, cherished and reassured in an instant.

For me, I *have* to start every single day with a cup of tea. I love the ritual of waking up, boiling the kettle and then sitting down, cup in hand and thinking about what I'm going to be doing that day. It's my little moment of calm before the madness of everyday life kicks in – the school run, homework time, long hours and the hundred and one other things that keep me running around in circles. And, as everyone knows, tea can help solve almost any problem! Whether it's a broken heart, a crisis at work or just 'one of those days', reaching for the kettle is halfway to making everything better. An afternoon cup of Earl Grey and all is right with the world! One of my very favourite things is my teapot – it's silver and shiny and I love to set it on the table with a cake cut into wedges or a plate of

biscuits. Or to curl up on my sofa with a big mug and take a step back from all the hustle and bustle. That's really the reason why I bake – so that I have something to eat with my cup of tea – and, as you can gather, I really, really love a cup of tea!

The recipes in this book are here for you to have fun with. I find that it can take a few goes to get something just how I like it, so don't worry if your baking looks a bit rough around the edges – it's all part of the charm. It'll taste delicious and I promise you won't hear any complaints! I also wanted to take a trip back to the time when I was little and teatime – as it was then, in the form of sandwiches and slices of cake – was a regular occurrence. I'm sure that, as we get older, our memories of childhood become rose-tinted, but those times that we really did have crumpets by the fire and cheese on toast followed by slices of Battenburg have stayed with me and etched themselves onto my memory, waiting to be recreated with my daughter. Billie and I love to spend time in the kitchen together cooking and just being with each other, and there are many recipes in this book that bring back lovely memories of afternoons spent playing with pastry and cookie dough. I love that something as simple as cake can create such lifelong memories down the generations and I want to pass that on through these recipes.

I love taking cookery books up to bed with me and reading them as I would a novel, but I often don't actually end up making things from many

of them. I really hope you will enjoy *using* this book! I would love to think that *Tea & Cake* will sit on your kitchen shelf, a little battered around the edges and covered in butter and icing and a load of chocolate fingerprints – a book that you can go to time and time again for inspiration and to bake something delicious, whether it's for your best friend who needs a shoulder to cry on, a surprise pitch-up of family on a Sunday afternoon, or a cake sale at your children's school that you only remembered at the last minute.

I remember once driving to a job halfway across the country. It was late, pouring with rain and the traffic was terrible. I stopped off to pick someone up and when I arrived at their house, tired and cold, I was greeted by a steaming cup of tea and homemade biscuits. It was exactly what I needed and I was overwhelmed by the warmth and kindness of this simple act. I couldn't stop thinking about it and it is what finally prompted me to write down all my recipes here for you to share. I think the moment was so very special to me because the person who demonstrated that love through her baking was one of my all-time heroes, Mary Berry. So thank you, Mary, for inspiring me to write this book.

A cake that can be cut into lots of pieces or a plate of biscuits ready for dunking into hot tea has been made with love, and that in itself is a truly special thing. Have fun with these recipes and make them your own – and remember: there is always time for another cup of tea!

Lisa x

NB: *Tea may be one of my favourite things in the world, but obviously feel free to substitute it with a hot drink of your choice!*

1

BISCUITS

DUNK!

A chapter dedicated almost entirely to perfect things to dunk! I used to think I wasn't really a baker. I'd say, 'But I don't bake! Yes, I make biscuits, cakes and pastries several times a week, but that's only so I have something to eat with a cup of tea!' So, on the following pages, you'll find some of my favourites for your mid-morning, mid-afternoon, or anytime tea break. ❧

№ 1

THE PERFECT DUNKER

✳

Properly crisp on the outside, squidgy and gooey inside, these all-American cookies are super-quick and easy – and perfect for dunking in your tea or hot milk! I make double the dough, roll it into cylinders, wrap it in cling film and freeze it because everybody loves them! Just slice into rounds, straight from the freezer, and bake them whenever you need a cookie fix.

MAKES 30

225 g (8 oz) unsalted butter, softened, plus extra for greasing

330 g (11½ oz) caster sugar

2 eggs

300 g (10½ oz) plain flour

2 teaspoons baking powder

1 teaspoon bicarbonate of soda

70 g (2¾ oz) cocoa powder

150 g (5 oz) chocolate chips

METHOD: Preheat the oven to 180°C (350°F), gas mark 4. Grease a baking tray with butter (or two if you don't have one large enough for 30 cookies) and line with greaseproof paper.

Beat the butter with an electric (hand) whisk until light and fluffy then beat in the sugar. Beat in the eggs one at a time, adding 1 tablespoon of the flour after each egg to prevent the mixture from splitting.

Sift together the remaining flour, baking powder, bicarbonate of soda and cocoa powder, then mix with the chocolate chips.

Slowly add the dry ingredients to the wet mixture. Scrape the bowl down again so that the ingredients are evenly mixed, then give one final stir to ensure everything is combined. The mixture will be quite dry; this is exactly what you want as you have to take heaped teaspoons and roll them into balls. Once all your balls are rolled, pop them on the baking tray, spaced a few inches apart, as they will spread. Pat the cookie balls to flatten slightly and bake for 12 minutes.

Transfer to a wire rack to cool.

TIP: You can use dark or white chocolate chips – or halve the dough and mix different colours into each batch.

№ 2

BUTTER COOKIES

When I was seventeen, I spent a lot of time working (or rather, not working but just going to castings and not getting jobs!) in Paris. I fell in love with the place almost immediately, and wandered the streets and sat in tabacs, watching the world go by and listening to the beautiful French language! One place I used to go to a lot was Mariage Frères, a teashop where they make the most fantastic tea in beautiful teapots. They also serve these biscuits, which reminded me of home and kept me going when I got homesick.

MAKES 15

150 g (5 oz) plain flour

30 g (1 oz) cornflour

20 g (¾ oz) custard powder

1 teaspoon baking powder

160 g (5½ oz) butter, softened

50 g (2 oz) icing sugar

¼ teaspoon vanilla extract

METHOD: Combine the plain flour, cornflour, custard powder and baking powder in a bowl. In another large mixing bowl, cream the butter and icing sugar until fluffy and pale using an electric mixer, then add the vanilla extract.

Sift in the flour mixture and beat with an electric mixer on low until thoroughly combined. Lightly knead into a dough. Cover in cling film and roll into a tube 3.5 cm (1½ inches) in diameter. Wrap up securely and refrigerate for 30 minutes to an hour, or until it is firm enough to slice.

Preheat the oven to 180°C (350°F), gas mark 4, and line one or two baking trays with greaseproof paper.

Remove the dough from the fridge and slice into 15 mm (⅝ inch) thick discs. Place on the baking trays, spacing them about 2 cm (¾ inch) apart.

Bake in the preheated oven for about 15 minutes, or until light brown. Remove from the oven and let them sit for 5 minutes. Transfer to a wire rack to cool down completely.

№ 3

CHOCOLATE BISCOTTI

✕

This is one for the coffee lovers out there. I love the smell of freshly ground coffee, but I have to say I don't really drink it. These are worth having a cup for, though, just to dunk the biscuit!

MAKES ABOUT 10

50 g (2 oz) butter, plus extra for greasing

110 g (4 oz) plain flour

½ teaspoon baking powder

20 g (¾ oz) cocoa powder

75 g (3 oz) soft brown sugar

30 g (1 oz) chocolate chips

30 g (1 oz) toasted flaked almonds

1 egg white

METHOD: Preheat the oven to 170°C (325°F), gas mark 3, and grease a baking tray with butter.

Sift the flour, baking powder and cocoa powder into the bowl of a food processor. Add the butter and sugar and pulse until the mixture resembles breadcrumbs.

Turn out into a large bowl, add the chocolate chips, almonds and egg white and knead together.

Shape the dough into a rough log shape and place on the prepared baking tray. Flatten it down just a little bit. Bake for 30 minutes.

Remove from the oven and leave to cool for 15 minutes on a wire rack. Turn down the oven to 160°C (320°F), gas mark 3. (The temperature change is very small, so if you're using a gas oven set it just below mark 3.)

Slice the loaf into about 10 biscotti, depending on how thick you'd like them – I like mine to be fairly thin. Place the pieces back on the baking tray and cook for 10–15 minutes, then turn them over and cook for a further 10–15 minutes until dry and crispy. Leave to cool on a wire rack.

№ 4

SABLÉ BISCUITS

These biscuits are super-light and crumbly and they make the perfect accompaniment to poached pears and chocolate sauce, or a fool or panna cotta. They are also great just on their own. If you want something less traditional, play around with the shape of these biscuits – crescent moons and stars work well!

MAKES 25–30

200 g (7 oz) plain flour
90 g (3¼ oz) caster sugar
60 g (2½ oz) ground almonds
200 g (7 oz) butter, diced
1 egg
zest of ½ lemon
2 drops vanilla extract
pinch of fine salt

METHOD: Put the flour, sugar and almonds in a food processor and blitz for a few seconds. Add the butter and work again until the mixture is just blended and resembles fine breadcrumbs. Add the whole egg, lemon zest, vanilla extract and salt and work again briefly until the dough forms into balls.

Scrape out on to a sheet of cling film and either shape into a rough ball or roll into a cylinder about 5 cm (2 inches) in diameter. Wrap and chill for at least 2 hours (you can freeze the dough or make it a few days ahead).

Preheat the oven to 190°C (375°F), gas mark 5.

Cut into 5 mm (¼ inch) discs or ovals and transfer to a flat baking sheet lined with greaseproof paper.

Bake in the preheated oven for 12 minutes, until a pale golden colour.

ALMOND THINS

I have made these and eaten the whole batch in one sitting while putting the world to rights with my best friends. The thing is, they are so deceptively thin and crispy that before you know it, all that's left is an empty plate!

MAKES ABOUT 36

115 g (4 oz) butter, cubed

300 g (10½ oz) demerara sugar

½ teaspoon ground cinnamon

80 ml (3 fl oz) water

325 g (11½ oz) plain flour

¼ teaspoon baking powder

85 g (3¼ oz) sliced blanched almonds

METHOD: Melt the butter in a medium-sized saucepan over a low heat along with the sugar, cinnamon and water. Stir until the butter just melts, but don't allow the ingredients to boil: most of the sugar should not be dissolved.

Remove from the heat and stir in the flour, baking powder and almonds until well mixed into a soft dough.

Line a 900 g (2 lb) loaf tin with cling film and press the dough into the tin so the top is smooth. Chill for about an hour or until firm.

Preheat the oven to 200°C (400°F), gas mark 6, and line a couple of baking sheets with greaseproof paper.

Using a very sharp knife, slice the dough crosswise, as thinly as possible, into rectangles. The thinner they are, the more delicate and crisp they'll be.

Space the rectangles on the prepared baking sheets and bake for 8 minutes, or until they look quite firm. Flip the thins over and bake for a further 8 minutes, until they are crisp and golden brown on top. The biscuits may take a little more or less time to cook depending on how thin you have cut them.

Cool completely, then store in an airtight container for up to 3 days until ready to serve. The unbaked dough can be stored in the refrigerator for up to 4 days, or frozen for up to 2 months, if well wrapped.

№ 6

GINGER BISCUITS

As teenagers my sister and I would come home from school, make rounds and rounds of toast and cups of tea, eat packets of ginger nuts and study at the same kitchen table I'm writing at today. In memory of those bittersweet days I give you the humble ginger biscuit! They are crispy and even more delicious because they are homemade.

MAKES 30

340 g (12 oz) plain flour, plus extra
   for dusting

2 heaped teaspoons ground ginger

¼ teaspoon ground cloves

100 g (3½ oz) soft light brown sugar

80 g (3 oz) caster sugar

100 g (3½ oz) cold salted butter

4 pieces stem ginger in syrup, finely
   chopped

2 tablespoons syrup from the stem
   ginger jar

2 tablespoons golden syrup

1 egg, beaten

demerara sugar, to sprinkle

METHOD: Line two flat baking sheets with greaseproof paper.

Sift the flour and spices into a large bowl and stir through the sugars. Add the butter and rub in with your fingertips until the mixture resembles breadcrumbs. Stir through the chopped ginger then mix in the syrups and beaten egg.

Turn the mixture out on to a lightly floured work surface and knead gently into a smooth dough. Wrap in cling film then refrigerate for 1 hour until firm. Roll out to a thickness of around 5 mm (¼ inch) then cut into discs using a 6 cm (2½ inch) straight-sided cutter. Lay on the prepared baking sheets, leaving a space of around 5 cm (2 inches) between each, then refrigerate for 30 minutes.

Preheat the oven to 180°C (350°F), gas mark 4. Sprinkle the biscuits with demerara sugar and bake for 10 minutes until golden brown, then reduce the heat to 150°C (300°F), gas mark 2, and bake for a further 10 minutes until crisp. Transfer to a wire rack to cool.

№ 7

BRETON CAKE

The first time I tried this cake, my cousins had brought it back from their camping holiday in France. It had obviously been sitting on the back seat of the car and most of it had been eaten on the long drive home, but there was a tiny bit left and I nabbed it! If you don't like butter this cake's not for you, but it's one of my favourites in this book!

SERVES 12

250 g (9 oz) best salted butter, softened, plus extra for greasing
225 g (8 oz) plain flour
250 g (9 oz) golden caster sugar, plus 1 teaspoon
5 egg yolks (reserve a couple of the whites to use as a glaze)

METHOD: Preheat the oven to 180°C (350°F), gas mark 4, and grease a 23 cm (9 inch) springform cake tin with butter.

Sift the flour into a bowl, add the butter, sugar and egg yolks and beat together to form a dough.

Pour into the cake tin and pat down or bang on a surface to flatten.

Mix the reserved egg whites with the teaspoon of sugar and a splash of water to make a glaze. Brush over the cake and cook for 30–40 minutes, until golden. Leave to cool slightly, then cut into pieces.

№ 8

ICED PARTY RINGS

✳

These colourful biscuits were another family favourite of the bought variety when I was growing up. They are great for children's parties, and Billie loves to decorate them with me.

MAKES 25–30

200 g (7 oz) plain flour

100 g (3½ oz) golden caster sugar

100 g (3½ oz) salted butter, softened

1 teaspoon vanilla extract

1 egg

FOR THE ICING

300 g (10½ oz) icing sugar, sifted

food colourings of your choice

METHOD: Mix together the flour and sugar. Add the butter and combine until the mixture resembles fine breadcrumbs. Add the vanilla extract and egg and bring together to form a dough. Cover with cling film and chill for about 30 minutes.

Preheat the oven to 180°C (350°F), gas mark 4, and line a baking tray with greaseproof paper.

Roll out the dough on a floured work surface to about 5 mm (¼ inch) thick and cut out 6 cm (2½ inch) circles. Then cut out and discard a 2 cm (¾ inch) circle from the middle of each biscuit. Place the rings on the prepared baking tray and chill again for about 10 minutes. Transfer to the oven and cook for 10 minutes, or until golden. Leave to cool on a wire rack.

Meanwhile, add just enough water to the icing sugar to make a thick, spreadable consistency (you will probably only need about a tablespoon). Divide into bowls according to how many colours you use – I usually do pink and yellow – and add the colouring of your choice.

Spread the icing on to the biscuits then, using a teaspoon, drizzle a contrasting colour over the top in a sort of zigzag pattern. Allow to set.

CHRISTMAS BISCUITS

✳

I love the little traditions that everyone has at Christmas time – the things that they do in their house that make it extra special. In our house it's the build-up that is so exciting for Billie and me: the cake- and pudding-making, and of course the Christmas biscuits! We make little holes in some of these biscuits before baking and then tie them to the Christmas tree with ribbons – believe me, they are not there long enough to go stale!

MAKES AROUND 30 (DEPENDING ON THE SIZE OF YOUR CUTTER)

250 g (9 oz) unsalted butter, plus
    extra for greasing
140 g (4¾ oz) dark brown muscovado
    sugar

1 egg yolk
300 g (10½ oz) plain flour
1 teaspoon mixed spice
1 teaspoon ground ginger

METHOD: Cream together the butter and sugar until pale and fluffy then mix in the egg yolk.

Stir together the flour and spices and fold into the creamed mixture until thoroughly incorporated. Wrap the dough in cling film and chill for at least 2 hours.

Preheat the oven to 180°C (350°F), gas mark 4, and grease a baking tray with butter.

Roll the dough out to about 5 mm (¼ inch) thick and cut into star shapes (or whatever shape you like!) using a 7 cm (2¾ inch) cutter. (At this point, use a skewer to make a little hole in each biscuit if you want to hang them up when cooked.)

Place the stars on the baking tray and chill in the fridge for about 30 minutes – this stops the biscuits from spreading.

Bake in the preheated oven for 12 minutes. Cool and decorate in any way you choose – for example, with coloured icing and silver balls – and hang with pretty ribbon.

> *TIP: Don't feel you can only make these at Christmas – get some different-shaped cutters and string them up at Easter, Halloween, birthdays… any occasion!*

'I'm a bit of a tea addict, but
my favourite is a cup of Earl
Grey with just the tiniest drop
of milk. Some people think
I'm fussy, but you know what,
it's important... a cup of tea,
just the way you like it!'

LISA

№ 10

SPONGE FINGERS

✦

The thing I love about these biscuits is how light they are – you can eat a load in one sitting! My mum used to give these to me instead of rusks when I was a toddler. I'm not sure what that says about either of us, but I still love them now…

MAKES 30

3 egg whites, plus 1 extra for
    decorating
pinch of salt
100 g (3½ oz) caster sugar, plus extra
    for sprinkling

6 egg yolks
100 g (3½ oz) plain flour, sifted
20 g (¾ oz) cornflour, sifted

METHOD: Preheat the oven to 200°C (400°F), gas mark 6, and line two baking sheets with greaseproof paper.

Beat the egg whites and salt with an electric hand whisk until stiff. Gradually whisk in half of the sugar until the egg whites are stiff and glossy then set aside. In a separate bowl beat the egg yolks and the remaining sugar until pale and doubled in volume; this will take 7–8 minutes with an electric whisk or stand mixer. Carefully fold in the egg whites a third at a time, then fold in the flour and cornflour, taking care to keep as much air in the mixture as possible.

Transfer the mixture to a large piping bag fitted with a 1 cm (½ inch) plain round nozzle and pipe on to the baking sheets in 5–6 cm (2–2½ inch) lengths, leaving plenty of space in between to allow for spreading. Bake for 4–5 minutes until golden brown. Brush with egg white and sprinkle with caster sugar then put back in the oven for a further 2 minutes until crisp. Transfer to a wire rack to cool before serving.

№ 11

GILLIAN'S FLAPJACKS

My mum's friend Gillian lived opposite us when we were growing up. Her daughter was the same age as my sister Victoria, so they played together and Gillian and my mum used to swap recipes and talk cooking. Gillian's flapjacks were legendary: buttery (do you sense a pattern developing here?!) and gooey. I managed to track down her email address and ask her for this lost, but not forgotten, recipe.

MAKES ABOUT 16

175 g (6 oz) butter, plus extra for greasing
125 g (4½ oz) demerera sugar
2 level tablespoons golden syrup
350 g (12 oz) rolled oats

METHOD: Preheat the oven to 160°C (320°F), gas mark 3, and grease and line a 20 cm (8 inch) square tin with greaseproof paper.

In a saucepan, slowly melt the butter, sugar and syrup. Add the oats and mix well.

Pour into the tin and cook in the preheated oven for 25 minutes.

Leave in the tin to cool for 10 minutes then mark into squares. Allow to cool completely before removing from the tin.

TIP: To ring the changes, try adding a few raisins, dried cherries or chocolate chips along with the oats.

ENERGY BARS

Nobody who knows me would believe that I have actually got into keeping fit, but I have! I have always loved yoga but now I spin every week too. These bars are great for an energy boost, and they also make a great breakfast if you're on the move.

MAKES 24

50 g (2 oz) butter, plus extra for greasing

6 sheets of edible rice paper

50 g (2 oz) treacle

50 g (2 oz) golden syrup

50 ml (2 fl oz) maple syrup

50 g (2 oz) sultanas

50 g (2 oz) raisins

50 g (2 oz) dried mixed fruit

50 g (2 oz) dried apple, roughly chopped

50 g (2 oz) dried figs, roughly chopped

50 g (2 oz) dried mango, roughly chopped

100 g (3½ oz) granola

100 g (3½ oz) porridge oats

50 g (2 oz) dried milk powder

METHOD: Grease a deep 20 x 30 cm (8 x 12 inch) baking tray and line with half of the rice paper. Preheat the oven to 180°C (350°F), gas mark 4.

Put the butter, treacle and golden and maple syrups in a small saucepan and bring to the boil. Remove from the heat and set aside.

Mix the dry ingredients together in a large bowl and then pour in the syrup mixture and combine well.

Tip the mixture into the prepared baking tray and smooth over the surface. Lay the rest of the rice paper on top. Bake for 20 minutes then remove from the oven and leave to cool in the tin before cutting into squares.

CELEBRATE!

Sometimes all you need is a steaming mug of tea and the last biscuit in the tin. But at other times I like to make my afternoon tea break into a bit more of a celebration! In this chapter are all the littlest things that you can pile up high in a bowl or on pretty plates and serve alongside your favourite teacups and saucers. They are the perfect size to pop into your mouth! These are as much of a pleasure to make as they are to eat, so invite some people over and enjoy these little mouthfuls of heaven.

№ 1

FONDANT FANCIES

✳

These were another of my favourite cakes when I was growing up, but the Mr Kipling variety! My mother never let us buy cakes, she always made them, so to us it was a treat to go to someone else's house and have a Mr Kipling fondant fancy. I wanted to try and make these myself… Luckily a friend of mine from Billie's school is a fantastic baker and makes beautiful wedding cakes, so when my first attempt went wrong I took all my ingredients round to her house and we spent the whole day perfecting them. It's the icing that's tricky: it has to be pretty thin, but the end result is well worth the effort.

MAKES 25

FOR THE CAKE

225 g (8 oz) margarine, softened,
    plus extra for greasing

225 g (8 oz) golden caster sugar

4 eggs

2 teaspoons vanilla extract

225 g (8 oz) self-raising flour

pinch of salt

FOR THE BUTTERCREAM

250 g (9 oz) unsalted butter, softened

300 g (10½ oz) icing sugar, sifted

1 teaspoon vanilla extract

FOR THE ICING

500 g (1 lb 2 oz) white fondant icing

1 tablespoon cocoa powder

red and yellow food colouring

icing sugar, for dusting

TO DECORATE

200 g (7 oz) icing sugar, sifted

1 tablespoon cocoa powder

METHOD: Preheat the oven to 180°C (350°F), gas mark 4, and grease and line a 20 cm (8 x 8 inch) square cake tin with greaseproof paper.

In a large bowl, cream the margarine and sugar until pale and fluffy then beat in the eggs, one at a time. Beat in the vanilla extract. Sift the flour and salt into a separate bowl then carefully fold into the batter. Spoon into the prepared tin and bake for 30 minutes until a skewer inserted into the centre of the cake comes out clean. Transfer to a wire rack to cool.

When the cake has cooled, trim the edges and cut into 25 even squares; set aside.

For the buttercream, beat the butter and icing sugar until smooth then beat in the vanilla extract. Spread the top and sides of each square of cake with a thin layer of buttercream then top each with an extra blob. Transfer to the fridge for 30 minutes until firm.

Continued overleaf

✄

Meanwhile divide the fondant icing into three. Combine the cocoa powder with ½ teaspoon water to make a paste then knead into one of the pieces of icing until smooth. Colour the other pieces of icing with the red and yellow food colourings so that you have one brown, one pink and one yellow piece of icing.

When you are ready to ice the cakes, remove 8 from the fridge (leave the remaining cakes in the fridge to keep them cold and firm so they are easier to work with). Dust the work surface with icing sugar and roll out the chocolate icing thinly. Cut into 8 squares, each large enough to cover a cake with some spare – like a tablecloth. Cover each cake neatly with the icing. Smooth it down the sides of the cake, then trim the edges. Transfer to a wire rack. Repeat with the remaining cakes and icing. This is quite tricky, but by the time you get to the last one you'll have got the hang of it!

To decorate, combine half of the icing sugar with just enough water to make a loose icing then spoon into a piping bag fitted with a fine plain nozzle. Repeat with the remaining icing sugar, but this time adding the cocoa powder. Pipe the white icing in lines over the pink cakes and the chocolate icing over the remaining cakes.

№ 2

COCONUT ICE

✻

When I think of this pink and white confection, memories of seventies children's tea parties go rushing through my head. It was also the classic sweet made by mums for school fêtes, and I remember buying bags of the stuff!

MAKES ABOUT 50 PIECES

butter, for greasing
1 x 397 g (14 oz) tin condensed milk
325 g (11½ oz) icing sugar

325 g (11½ oz) desiccated or
   shredded coconut
few drops of pink food colouring

METHOD: Grease a 22 cm (8½ inch) square tin with butter and line it with cling film, then grease the cling film too.

Mix together the condensed milk, icing sugar and coconut. Take half the mixture and press it into the tin. Add a few drops of pink food colouring to the remaining half of the mixture and then press it down on top of the white mixture in the tin.

Cover and leave to set, preferably overnight, before cutting into squares.

NOTE: This makes a lot, but it keeps for a really long time. I like to keep mine in the fridge so it stays cool – I just can't resist going back for one more piece...

LEMON MERINGUE SANDWICH COOKIES

✳

Pretty and tasty and perfect for a tea party, these biscuits are a real winner! They are also very easy to make and great served as a pud. Try making your own lemon curd (see page 196) or you can use shop-bought.

MAKES 12

FOR THE BISCUITS

250 g (9 oz) plain flour

100 g (3½ oz) rice flour

250 g (9 oz) salted butter, softened

75 g (3 oz) golden caster sugar

finely grated zest of 1 lemon

1 egg yolk

FOR THE FILLING

200 ml (7 fl oz) double cream

3 tablespoons lemon curd

4 meringue shells, crushed

METHOD: Sift the flours into a large bowl and make a well in the centre. Add the butter, sugar, lemon zest and egg yolk. Gradually work in the flour using your fingertips until the mixture comes together to form a soft dough. Wrap in cling film and chill for 30 minutes until firm.

Preheat the oven to 150°C (300°F), gas mark 2, and line a baking sheet with greaseproof paper.

Dust the work surface with a little flour and roll out the dough to a thickness of 5 mm (¼ inch). Cut into discs with a 6 cm (2½ inch) round cutter and place on the prepared baking sheet. Refrigerate for 30 minutes until firm.

Bake the biscuits for about 30 minutes until a pale golden colour, then transfer to a wire rack to cool.

Meanwhile, whisk the cream to soft peaks then fold through the lemon curd and crushed meringue. Spoon the mixture onto half of the biscuits then sandwich with the remaining plain biscuits.

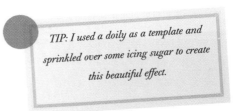

TIP: I used a doily as a template and sprinkled over some icing sugar to create this beautiful effect.

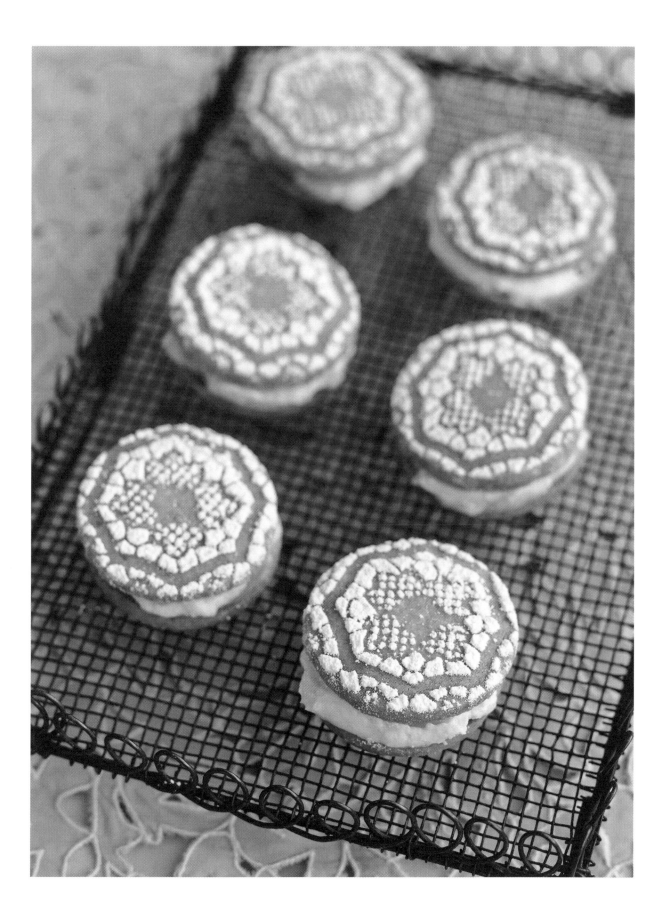

FLORENTINES

✄

I love these biscuits – they used to intrigue me when I was little and spied them in confectioners' shop windows while on holiday in France. They also make a great gift.

MAKES 15–20

30 g (1 oz) butter

75 g (3 oz) golden caster sugar

30 g (1 oz) plain flour, plus extra
for dusting

50 g (2 oz) ready-flaked almonds

25 g (1 oz) glacé cherries, chopped

25 g (1 oz) sour cherries, chopped

50 g (2 oz) crystallised ginger,
chopped

150 g (5 oz) dark chocolate, broken
into pieces

METHOD: Preheat the oven to 190°C (375°F), gas mark 5.

Melt the butter and sugar with the flour in a saucepan over a low heat. Add the almonds, cherries and ginger and stir through.

Take off the heat and roll teaspoon-sized balls of the mixture on to a baking tray lined with greaseproof paper, spacing them apart as they will spread in the oven. Flatten them down with the back of a spoon. I like my Florentines small and thin! You may need a few baking trays.

Bake in the oven for 12–15 minutes.

Remove from the oven and leave the Florentines to cool on the tray.

Meanwhile, melt the chocolate in a bowl set over a pan of simmering water (make sure the bottom of the bowl doesn't actually touch the hot water). Once cooled, turn the Florentines over and brush the bottoms with the melted chocolate. When set, turn them back over and drizzle a little melted chocolate over the top.

> TIP: Classic Florentines are meant to spread and have a frilly edge, but if you want really neat rounds, spread the mixture on to a baking tray lined with greaseproof paper and cook for 10–12 minutes until golden. Leave to cool on the tray for 10 minutes, then peel off the sheet and use a cutter to cut out tidy circles before brushing with melted chocolate.

№ 5

CHERRY & ALMOND TARTLETS

I have always said how very blessed I feel to work with such talented and special people. On *What's Cooking?* I became friends with the lovely Rachel Allen. Among other delicious things, she made little rhubarb tarts with an almond pastry. They were really simple and very delicious and that night I went home and recreated them with cherries.

MAKES 12

50 g (2 oz) unsalted butter, plus
    extra for greasing
½ teaspoon vanilla bean paste
50 g (2 oz) caster sugar
50 g (2 oz) ground almonds
FOR THE CHERRIES
12 ripe cherries, stoned

50 g (2 oz) caster sugar
2 tablespoons kirsch
1 teaspoon vanilla extract
TO SERVE
100 ml (3½ fl oz) double cream,
    whipped to soft peaks

METHOD: Preheat the oven to 180°C (350°F), gas mark 4, and grease a 12-hole mince pie tray (or shallow bun tin). Cream the butter and vanilla paste in a bowl using an electric hand mixer. Add the caster sugar and ground almonds, then stir to combine – do not beat. Place 2 full teaspoons of the mixture – no need to spread – in each hole of the mince pie tray and bake for about 6–10 minutes, until a deep golden colour. Keep an eye on them as they burn easily! Let them sit in the tin for 2 minutes before removing to a wire tray to cool. If they cool completely in the tin, they will stick. If that happens, just pop them back in the oven for 1 minute.

Meanwhile, put the cherries, sugar, kirsch, vanilla extract and 2 tablespoons of water into a saucepan. Bring to the boil then simmer for 2 minutes until the cherries start to soften. Remove the cherries from the pan with a slotted spoon and transfer to a bowl. Bring the liquid back to the boil and cook for 3–4 minutes until thick and syrupy. Pour the syrup over the cherries and leave to cool completely.

Spoon or pipe a little whipped cream onto each tartlet and top with a cherry and a little of the syrup.

TURKISH DELIGHT

✖

Anyone who knows me knows that I don't drink coffee, and for years I didn't like Turkish delight. . . until I went to my Turkish friend Sibel's house. She made Turkish breakfast and afterwards Turkish coffee served with Turkish delight. The coffee was thick and sweet and, though not my favourite, I was fascinated by it. The Turkish delight was so delicately flavoured that I went straight home and made some. Many modern Turkish delight recipes use gelatine, which gives it a slightly different texture. This recipe uses the good old-fashioned method. It requires a lot of love as the mixture needs a good deal of stirring but, trust me, it's worth it!

MAKES ABOUT 60 PIECES

1–2 tablespoons lemon juice

800 g (1 lb 12 oz) caster sugar

1 teaspoon cream of tartar

120 g (5 oz) cornflour

1–2 tablespoons rosewater

few drops of red/pink food colouring

TO DUST

160 g (6 oz) icing sugar

30 g (1 oz) cornflour

METHOD: Bring 350 ml (12 fl oz) water, the lemon juice and sugar to the boil in a saucepan over a low to medium heat, stirring all the time. Continue boiling and stirring until the mixture reaches 115°C (240°F). Turn the heat off and set the pan aside.

In another saucepan, heat 500 ml (16 fl oz) water, the cream of tartar and cornflour. With an electric hand mixer whisk the mixture as it comes to the boil and forms a consistency like wallpaper paste, gluey and sticky. Take off the heat.

Little by little, add the sugar syrup to the white paste and whisk with your electric mixer. Bring to the boil then turn the heat down and very gently simmer for about 1 hour. You must stir this pretty much continuously, every 5 minutes or so. The mixture will turn a beautiful amber colour. Add the rosewater and food colouring, and mix together.

Oil a 22 cm (8½ inch) square tin and line with cling film, then oil the cling film too. Pour the mixture into the tin, cover and leave to cool completely, preferably overnight.

The next day turn the tin out on to a board dusted with icing sugar, peel off the cling film and dust with icing sugar.

Mix and sift together into a bowl the remaining icing sugar and cornflour. Cut the Turkish delight into squares and toss in the icing sugar mix. Store in an airtight jar.

№ 7

LITTLE JAM PUFFS

✳

These were one of my favourite biscuits when I was younger. I remember enjoying a lemon version of them too. The sugar syrup on the puff pastry makes them go all crispy and the jam is a little sharp, while being sticky and chewy. They are fun to make and look really pretty – sort of like a delicate jammy dodger!

MAKES 12–14

375 g (13 oz) ready-rolled puff pastry
splash of milk
3 tablespoons redcurrant jelly
3 tablespoons raspberry jam

small squeeze (2 teaspoons) lemon juice
2 gelatine leaves
2 tablespoons caster sugar

METHOD: Preheat the oven to 200°C (400°F), gas mark 6. Line a baking sheet with greaseproof paper and cut a second sheet the same size. Unroll the pastry sheet and cut off one-third of the pastry. Roll this smaller piece of pastry as thin as possible between two sheets of greaseproof paper then use a 4.5 cm (1¾ inch) fluted cutter to cut out 12–14 circles and place them on the lined baking sheet.

Take the second, larger piece of puff pastry and cut out 12–14 discs using the 4.5 cm (1¾ inch) fluted cutter then cut a 2.5 cm (1 inch) circle from the centre of each of these using a plain cutter. Brush the rings with a little milk and place them (milk-side down) on top of the thinner discs on the baking sheet. Top with the second piece of greaseproof paper. Place a second baking sheet on top (try not to use one that is very heavy – a light baking sheet will keep the pastry compressed but allow it to rise a little) and bake in the oven for 12–15 minutes until the pastry is golden brown and a little puffed. If the centres of the puffs have risen up push them down gently with your finger.

Meanwhile, heat the redcurrant jelly and raspberry jam together in a small pan with 1 tablespoon of water. Sieve the mixture into a bowl then wash out the pan before returning the jam mixture to the heat and letting it bubble for a couple of minutes. Add the lemon juice, remove from the heat and pour into a bowl. Soften the gelatine leaves in a small bowl of cold water then squeeze out all the excess water and add them to the hot jam mixture. Stir until dissolved then set aside.

Melt the caster sugar in a very small pan with 2 tablespoons of water and allow to bubble until you have a light syrup. When cooled, it should feel like Vaseline when you rub a little between your fingers.

Once the puffs are out of the oven, spoon a little of the cooling jam mixture into their centres and brush all over the pastry with the sugar syrup. Leave to cool completely before serving.

№ 8

ORANGE BLOSSOM
BAKLAVA

◈

I couldn't do a sweet book without including one of the sweetest, stickiest treats of all time: layers of crispy filo with gooey, syrupy butter and just a hint of orange blossom – perfection! My friend Katie is Greek and we recently spent one Saturday morning making mountains of baklava and drinking tea. Her motto is: 'We're Greek, we always cook too much food!'

MAKES ABOUT 20

175 g (6 oz) clarified butter, melted

200 g (7 oz) ready-made filo pastry

200 g (7 oz) chopped almonds

200 g (7 oz) chopped pistachios

FOR THE SYRUP

300 g (10½ oz) caster sugar

60 ml (2½ fl oz) honey

1 teaspoon vanilla extract

a few drops of orange blossom water

METHOD: Preheat the oven to 180°C (350°F), gas mark 4. Brush an 18 x 28 cm (7 x 11 inch) baking tray with butter and cut the pastry sheets to fit.

Mix the nuts together. Layer sheets of filo on the baking tray one by one, brushing each with melted butter and sprinkling over some nut mixture. Continue to layer the filo, butter and nuts until 4 sheets of filo remain. Brush each of these final layers with melted butter before laying on top of the others. Once finished, score the top into diamond shapes and brush with the remaining melted butter. Bake for 30–40 minutes until golden.

Meanwhile, put the sugar and honey in a pan with 225 ml (8 fl oz) water, and bring to the boil slowly until the sugar has dissolved. Simmer without stirring for 5 minutes, then stir in the vanilla extract and a few drops of orange blossom water.

Take the baklava out of the oven and immediately pour over the syrup. Let it cool completely in the tin before cutting into diamonds and serving.

TIP: If you like cinnamon, mix ½ teaspoon with the nuts before layering with the pastry.

№ 9

PISTACHIO & ROSE BRITTLE

One of the things I love about today is that by the power of Twitter and Instagram the world has become a smaller place, and I have been lucky enough to befriend people from far and wide. I follow somebody called Clementine from Australia. I love her tweets and her food photos and if she lived in London I'd want to hang out with her! This is one of her recipes. You can get dried rose petals in many places now, and they are really pretty. However, you could simply leave them out and either add a little rosewater or just have pistachio brittle.

MAKES 500 G (1 LB 2 OZ)

200 g (7 oz) unsalted shelled pistachios	½ teaspoon bicarbonate of soda
330 g (11½ oz) caster sugar	pinch of sea salt
50 g (2 oz) unsalted butter	grated zest of 1 orange
125 ml (4 fl oz) water	1½ teaspoons ground cardamom
	10 dried rosebuds, petals separated

METHOD: Preheat the oven to 160°C (320°F), gas mark 3. Roast the pistachios on a baking tray for 10–12 minutes, shaking the tray frequently – you don't want them to colour, just dry out a little. Tip into a bowl and cool.

Line a baking tray with greaseproof paper. Combine the caster sugar, butter and water in a heavy-based saucepan over a low heat until the sugar dissolves. Increase the heat to bring to a boil and cook over a medium heat for 15–20 minutes until the mixture is a light golden caramel – if using a sugar thermometer, at 160°C (320°F) it will be approaching the hard crack stage. Remove from the heat and immediately stir in the bicarbonate of soda, salt, orange zest, cardamom and roasted pistachios.

Scrape the mixture on to the prepared baking tray and use a spatula to smooth it out as thinly as you can. Sprinkle with rose petals, pressing them gently into the surface of the brittle. Leave to cool completely before breaking into pieces with a rolling pin.

MADELEINES

✳

I think I may have mentioned in *The Way I Cook*… a French exchange I went on when I was fourteen. It wasn't my finest moment, lots went wrong over there, but one of the things I adored was my French breakfast every morning. It consisted of a bowl of hot chocolate and a plate of madeleines. I have tried lots of recipes for these over the years, and finally I am happy with this one. Almost crispy when they first come out of the oven, once stored in an airtight container the madeleines take on that stickiness that I love. I sometimes warm the madeleine tray up first because I think it enhances the crispy outside. I also like to add a teaspoon of vanilla extract. The tins are pretty easy to get hold of so don't be put off – you will use it again and again!

MAKES 10–12

2 eggs

100 g (3½ oz) caster sugar

125 g (4½ oz) plain flour, plus extra
    for dusting

1 small teaspoon baking powder

70 g (2¾ oz) butter, melted and
    cooled, plus extra for greasing

25 ml (1 fl oz) milk

METHOD: Preheat the oven to 200°C (400°F), gas mark 6.

Whisk the eggs and sugar until they are light and fluffy, and the whisk leaves a ribbon pattern in the mixture when you lift it up. It needs to increase in volume by almost double. This takes about 6 minutes in a stand mixer on high.

Lightly fold in all the other ingredients. Leave to stand for 20 minutes.

Brush the madeleine tray with melted butter, leave to set, then dust with a little flour, knocking out any excess. Gently spoon or pipe the madeleine batter into the moulds and bake for 8–10 minutes until lightly golden. Allow to cool in the tin for 5 minutes then turn out on to a wire rack to cool completely.

'There's nothing better
than having a good natter
with friends. Just make
a big pot of tea and a
huge plate of pretty sweet
things and it will be an
afternoon well spent!'

LISA

№ 11

MERINGUES WITH RHUBARB CREAM

✳

A different take on one of my mum's classic recipes. Meringues are one of my all-time favourite treats and the sharp rhubarb takes that edge off the sweetness. A tip: Never make meringues on stormy days – they just don't work!

MAKES 8

4 egg whites

300 g (10½ oz) caster sugar

1 teaspoon white wine vinegar

300 g (10½ oz) rhubarb, washed and
    finely sliced

zest of 1 orange plus juice of ½ an
    orange

300 ml (½ pint) double cream

1 tablespoon icing sugar

1 vanilla pod, split open and seeds
    scraped out

METHOD: Preheat the oven to 130°C (260°F), gas mark ½, and line two baking trays with greaseproof paper.

Whisk the egg whites with an electric hand whisk until soft peaks form, then gradually whisk in 250 g (9 oz) of the sugar until the mixture is stiff and glossy. Add the vinegar and fold in.

Spoon the mixture on to the lined baking sheets to make 16 quenelles.

Bake in the preheated oven for 1 hour then turn the oven off. Keep the meringues in the oven for a further 30 minutes until crisp, and then transfer to a wire rack to cool.

Meanwhile, put the rhubarb, remaining caster sugar, orange zest and juice into a saucepan. Bring to the boil and simmer for 2–3 minutes until the rhubarb is soft. Remove from the heat and leave to cool.

In a bowl, whisk together the cream, icing sugar and vanilla seeds to soft peaks. Fold the cooled rhubarb into the cream.

When the meringues are cool, sandwich them together with the rhubarb cream.

TIP: *A little chopped fresh mint is lovely stirred through the rhubarb and cream at the end.*

№ 12

CHOUX HEARTS
WITH SUMMER BERRIES

These are the perfect little heart-shaped treats for your loved ones. As well as an almost healthy afternoon indulgence, I like to make them for pudding for a dinner party.

MAKES 8

FOR THE CHOUX PASTRY
90 g (3¼ oz) butter
360 ml (12½ fl oz) water
pinch each of salt and sugar
110 g (4 oz) plain flour, sifted

3 whole eggs, beaten well

TO SERVE
500 ml (18 fl oz) whipped cream
400 g (14 oz) mixed fresh berries

METHOD: Preheat the oven to 200°C (400°F), gas mark 6. Put the butter and water in a medium saucepan, add the salt and sugar, and bring to the boil. Make sure the butter is melted.

Remove from the heat, add the sifted flour all at once and really beat it in with a wooden spoon until the mixture comes away from the sides of the pan. Return to the heat and cook for 2 minutes until the paste is pale. Cool a little.

Add the beaten eggs, a little at a time, incorporating fully with a wooden spoon after each addition. The mixture will go glossy then back to dull. Add the eggs until the mixture is shiny again and it JUST drops off the wooden spoon. Cool the mixture for about 10 minutes.

Put in a piping bag and pipe heart shapes on to a baking sheet dampened with a little water.

Bake in the preheated oven for 15–20 minutes then reduce the temperature to 160°C (320°F), gas mark 3, and bake for a further 15–20 minutes until golden.

When cooked, turn the hearts over and pop back into the oven for 2 minutes to dry out a little. Split each heart in half horizontally and then spoon or pipe whipped cream on the base. Top with the other half and fill the centre with the fruit. Serve immediately.

№ 13

LEMON POSSET WITH
LAVENDER SHORTBREAD

◈

I included this posset not only because it's delicious but because I found some beautiful 'custard cups' in an antiques shop and asked what they were. They are tiny and apparently used for individual custards but I thought the posset would be perfect for them. Sometimes after dinner you just want a couple of spoonfuls of something sweet and this is ideal. Serve with lavender shortbread on the side.

SERVES 6

300 ml (½ pint) double cream

75 g (3 oz) caster sugar

juice and zest of 1–2 lemons

FOR THE LAVENDER SHORTBREAD

50 g (2 oz) lavender sugar

50 g (2 oz) caster sugar

175 g (6 oz) unsalted butter

250 g (9 oz) plain flour

pinch of salt

METHOD: Put the cream and caster sugar in a saucepan and slowly bring to the boil. Simmer, stirring continuously, for 3 minutes. Take off the heat and whisk in the lemon juice and zest to taste.

Pour into six 60 ml (2½ fl oz) glasses or custard cups and, when cool, refrigerate for at least 2 hours.

To make the lavender shortbread, preheat the oven to 190°C (375°F), gas mark 5.

Tip all the ingredients into a food processor and pulse until the dough comes together. Wrap it in cling film and chill in the fridge for 30 minutes.

Roll out the dough to a thickness of 8 mm (⅓ inch) and then cut out leaf shapes. Bake in the oven for 10 minutes. Allow to cool and serve with the chilled lemon posset.

TIP: You can buy lavender sugar, but it's really easy to make your own. Just pop a few dried buds of edible lavender in a jar of caster sugar. It will be ready overnight and last for up to six months.

TIP: If you don't have a special leaf-shaped cutter, use a round cutter to cut one side of the leaf and then the other.

3 CAKES

TAKE A
SLICE!

For me, cooking is all about sharing and this especially applies to cakes – you don't (often!) make a cake to eat by yourself! My mum and my grandmothers always had a tin in the kitchen with some sort of cake 'on the go' and I've definitely followed in their footsteps. I think even the actual process of making a cake is a bit of an event and so there are lots of ideas in this chapter – from loaf cakes to cake sale bakes and showier celebration cakes – to be enjoyed at every cake moment.

№ 1

EASY VICTORIA SPONGE

✳

I first made a Victoria sponge for my Girl Guides baking badge and it's one of those recipes that's fab because you can always remember it! Weigh the eggs in their shells and then just add the same amount of butter, sugar and flour. Perfect for every occasion – in summer I like to add fresh strawberries.

SERVES 8–10

3 large eggs

unsalted butter, softened, plus extra
    for greasing

golden caster sugar

self-raising flour

pinch of salt

1 teaspoon vanilla extract

1 tablespoon milk

TO SERVE

200 ml (7 fl oz) double cream

2 tablespoons icing sugar, plus extra
    for dusting

150 g (5 oz) raspberry jam

METHOD: Preheat the oven to 170°C (325°F), gas mark 3, and grease and line two 20 cm (8 inch) sandwich tins with greaseproof paper. Weigh the eggs (in their shells), then weigh out the same amount of butter, sugar and flour. In a large bowl, cream the butter and sugar until pale and fluffy, then beat in the eggs, one at a time. Sift the flour and salt into a bowl and carefully fold into the batter. Fold in the vanilla and milk, divide the batter between the two cake tins and smooth the tops with the back of a spoon.

Bake for 25–30 minutes until a skewer inserted into the centre comes out clean. Transfer to a wire rack to cool.

Meanwhile, whisk the cream and icing sugar to soft peaks. When the cakes are completely cool, turn one of them upside down on to a serving plate or board. Spread with the jam and spoon the cream over the top. Top with the second cake, dust with icing sugar and serve.

TIP: I used a doily and cut a heart out of the middle then dusted the cake with icing sugar – you can obviously cut out any shape you like!

LEMON DRIZZLE CAKE

✳

This is one of my sister Victoria's failsafe cakes. As I write this I have just come off the phone after a long conversation with her about what she can make for dinner this week. We are constantly chatting about what to cook, what to wear and what to do with the children at the weekend – and a slice of this light lemony cake and a cup of tea (of course) is the perfect accompaniment to our constant nattering. She likes to cook but doesn't love it, so anything she makes has to be easy and quick and something the whole family will enjoy. This ticks all the boxes!

MAKES 1 LARGE LOAF

125 g (4½ oz) butter, softened, plus extra for greasing

175 g (6 oz) caster sugar

175 g (6 oz) self-raising flour

4 tablespoons milk

2 large eggs

zest and juice of 2 lemons

5–6 rounded tablespoons icing sugar

METHOD: Preheat the oven to 180°C (350°F), gas mark 4. Grease a 900 g (2 lb) loaf tin with butter and line it with a strip of greaseproof paper along its length and up the short sides – leave some paper hanging over the edges so you can lift out the loaf easily once it is cooked.

In a large bowl, cream together the butter and sugar until pale and fluffy, then mix in the flour, milk, eggs and lemon zest.

Pour the mixture into the prepared tin and bake for 30–40 minutes. Remove the cake from the oven but leave it in the tin.

Heat the lemon juice in a small saucepan. Add the icing sugar and stir to dissolve.

Using a skewer, make a few holes in the cake, then pour over the lemon juice mixture and leave to cool in the tin before turning out.

TIP: I particularly like eating the end slices – they're extra crunchy and sweet!

№ 3

YOGURT CAKE

✳

This is one of John Torode's recipes. I asked him for it several times just to hear his pronunciation of the word 'yogurt', which always makes me smile! My mum used to make cakes in ring moulds and I use hers today for this. If you're not a fan of yogurt, don't worry; you can't actually taste it – it just gives the cake a great moist texture.

SERVES 10–12

FOR THE PLUMS

4 or 5 plums, split and stoned

200 g (7 oz) caster sugar

zest and juice of 1 orange

2 cloves

1 vanilla pod, split open and seeds
    scraped out

FOR THE CAKE

120 ml (4 fl oz) yogurt

300 g (10½ oz) flour

150 g (5 oz) caster sugar

80 ml (3 fl oz) corn oil

2 teaspoons baking powder

2 eggs

METHOD: Place the plums, sugar, orange zest and juice, cloves, vanilla seeds and pod in a saucepan and cover with water. Bring to the boil and simmer for 3 minutes. Turn off the heat but leave in the pan to soften.

Preheat the oven to 180°C (350°F), gas mark 4, and grease a 35 cm (14 inch) ring cake tin with a little margarine or oil.

Place all the cake ingredients in a mixing bowl and stir well to remove any lumps. You can use a whisk to help smooth it out. Pour half of the cake batter into the tin. Drain the plums well, reserving the liquid, and place them all around the ring mould. Top with the rest of the cake batter.

Put on the centre shelf of the oven and cook for about 20 minutes until golden brown.

Meanwhile, put the reserved plum liquid into a saucepan and bring to the boil. Reduce by half, then strain (keep the vanilla pod and add it to a jar of sugar to make vanilla sugar) and place back over the heat to reduce to a syrup.

Leave the cake to cool for 5–10 minutes then turn out the cake onto a serving plate. Serve the warm syrup poured over the cake.

TIP: Don't worry if cracks form in the sponge – you can just fill them with the plum syrup.

TIP: You don't have to use plums; you can use any soft fruit you like – I've even used tinned peaches, which work brilliantly!

№ 4

PAT'S BANANA CAKE

This recipe is from my godmother, Pat. She swears by it and says it's not like any other banana cake – and she's right. It is a cake, as opposed to a banana loaf, so it's a lot lighter, more 'cakey' and has three delicious layers.

SERVES 10–12

375 g (13 oz) self-raising flour
¼ teaspoon baking powder
175 g (6 oz) soft margarine, plus extra for greasing
375 g (13 oz) caster sugar
3 eggs
3 large ripe bananas, peeled and mashed
½ teaspoon vanilla extract
1½ teaspoons bicarbonate of soda
75 ml (3 fl oz) buttermilk

FOR THE ICING

50 g (2 oz) softened butter
125 g (4½ oz) soft cream cheese
1 medium or large ripe banana, peeled and mashed
½ teaspoon vanilla extract
800 g (1 lb 12 oz) icing sugar

METHOD: Preheat the oven to 180°C (350°F), gas mark 4. Grease and line three 23 cm (9 inch) round sandwich tins with greaseproof paper.

Sift together the flour and baking powder. In another bowl, cream the margarine and sugar until light and fluffy. Using an electric whisk on a very low setting, whisk in the eggs, bananas and vanilla extract.

Mix the bicarbonate of soda with the buttermilk and stir – it will start to rise instantly so use a large mug or glass. Add this to the batter alternately with the flour, each time whisking the mixture just enough to combine.

Divide the mixture between the three cake tins and bake in the oven for 25–30 minutes. The cake will start to smell strongly when cooked. To test the cake, gently press the middle with your finger – the indentation should disappear. If in doubt give the cake a little longer – it's better to be overcooked than undercooked!

Remove from the tins while still warm and leave to cool on a wire rack.

To make the icing, cream together the butter and cream cheese. Beat in the banana and vanilla extract. Add the icing sugar and beat in until the mixture is stiff enough to spread.

Continued overleaf

Spoon it into a piping bag fitted with a 1 cm (½ inch) plain round nozzle. (Leftover icing can be stored in a sealed container in the fridge, or frozen until required.)

Place one cooled cake on a large plate and pipe dots evenly all around the edge – this will give it a pretty finish once you've layered all the cakes. Spread a layer of icing in the middle. Top with a second cake and repeat the icing on top. Finish with the final cake and then pipe and spread icing all over the top.

NOTE: This is a very big cake! Not one for dainty slices…

BATTENBURG

I love Battenburg and was desperate to learn how to make one. My friend Helen, who is a fantastic baker and has her own celebration cake business, said she would help me, and we spent a happy summer's day playing about with this until we got it right. Helen swears by using margarine not butter for a lighter cake, but feel free to use half and half or all butter. I also recommend using Sugarflair cake colouring – it honestly makes a difference. When I tried this sponge with normal supermarket cake colouring it came out a weird brown colour!

SERVES 8–10

225 g (8 oz) margarine, plus extra for
   greasing
225 g (8 oz) sugar
4 eggs
225 g (8 oz) self-raising flour
¼ teaspoon Sugarflair pink colouring

1 teaspoon rosewater
1 teaspoon vanilla extract
350 g (12 oz) marzipan, plus a tiny
   drop of Sugarflair pink colouring
150 g (5 oz) apricot jam
icing sugar, for dusting

METHOD: Preheat the oven to 180°C (350°F), gas mark 4, and grease and line a 20 cm (8 inch) square cake tin with greaseproof paper.

Make a divider out of baking paper to separate the two sponges – it needs to be as high as the tin and doubled over for extra strength. Set it across the middle of the tin.

Beat together the margarine and sugar until light and fluffy. Gradually beat in the eggs, one at a time, adding a spoonful of flour if the mixture curdles. Fold in the remaining flour.

Weigh your cake mixture and divide it in half. To one half add the pink colouring and rosewater, and to the other half add the vanilla extract – try to fold them in so as not to knock out all the air.

Pour the two mixtures into either side of the prepared tin. Bake for 35–40 minutes until the cake springs back when lightly pressed.

Remove from the oven and leave to cool on a wire rack.

Meanwhile, prepare the marzipan. Dust the work surface with icing sugar and knead the marzipan, adding the tip of a cocktail stick of Sugarflair pink colouring. Knead until you get the colour you want, then roll out into a rectangle about 5 mm (¼ inch) thick, keeping your work surface dusted with icing sugar so it doesn't stick.

Continued overleaf

Trim both cakes to make sure they are the same size and cut each in half lengthways so that you have two strips of each colour. Warm the apricot jam in a saucepan or microwave. Lay a strip of pink cake on a board and glaze the top and sides with jam then put a plain sponge strip alongside it and glaze in the same way. Finish with the other strips on top so you have a chequerboard pattern. Brush the whole cake with the glaze then place it on the marzipan, at one end of the rectangle. Fold the marzipan over to encase the cake and trim the edges.

№ 6

ORANGE ALMOND CAKE
WITH PASSION FRUIT ICING

This is another recipe from my lovely Twitter friend, Clementine (see page 64 for her amazing pistachio and rose brittle). She posted the most beautiful photo of this cake (see page 95) and I just had to get in touch with her and ask for the recipe. Thank you, Clementine!

SERVES 8–10

melted butter, for greasing

2 oranges

3 eggs

215 g (7½ oz) caster sugar

300 g (10½ oz) ground almonds

1 teaspoon baking powder

FOR THE ICING

250 g (9 oz) cream cheese

300 g (10½ oz) icing sugar

3 large passion fruit (pulp only)

50–125 g (2–4½ oz) unsalted butter, softened (optional)

edible flowers, to decorate (optional)

METHOD: Preheat the oven to 170°C (325°F), gas mark 3. Lightly grease a 22 cm (8½ inch) springform tin with melted butter and line the base with greaseproof paper.

Place the oranges in a small saucepan and cover with water. Bring to the boil over a medium heat. Cook for 15 minutes or until tender. Drain the oranges and return to the pan. Cover with cold water and bring to the boil again. Simmer for 15 minutes and drain.

Coarsely chop the oranges, and remove and discard any seeds. Place the orange chunks in a food processor and process until smooth.

Whisk the eggs and sugar with an electric mixer until thick and pale. Gently fold in the orange purée, ground almonds and baking powder until just combined.

Pour into the prepared tin and bake for 1 hour or until a skewer inserted into the centre comes out clean. Leave in the tin for 20 minutes then turn out on to a wire rack to cool completely.

To make the icing, blend the cream cheese with the icing sugar and passion fruit pulp. If you want a smoother, richer icing, you can add some unsalted butter. Smooth over the cake once cooled and decorate with the flowers, if using.

NOTE: This cake looks amazing but it is SO simple. You just pour the icing over the top!

№ 7

ANGEL CAKE

It's funny how cakes go in and out of fashion. Not long ago I was having a conversation about this book and saying I would love to include angel cake, and at the time nobody knew what it was. Then six months later the cake turned up as a challenge on *The Great British Bake Off*! You think you have a great idea, but they've all been done before! It's a very light cake and you need the proper cake mould, but it really is super-impressive.

SERVES 8–10

butter, for greasing
115 g (4 oz) plain flour
85 g (3¼ oz) icing sugar
8 large egg whites, at room temperature
¼ teaspoon salt
1 teaspoon cream of tartar
150 g (5 oz) caster sugar
1 teaspoon vanilla extract

FOR THE ICING

3 large egg whites, at room temperature
150 g (5 oz) caster sugar
¼ teaspoon cream of tartar
2 tablespoons water
½ teaspoon coconut extract (see note)

TO SERVE

250 g (9 oz) desiccated coconut
400 g (14 oz) strawberries, cut into quarters, or blueberries

---

METHOD: Preheat the oven to 180°C (350°F), gas mark 4, and grease a 25 cm (10 inch) angel cake tin. Sift the flour and icing sugar into a large bowl and set aside.

Tip the egg whites and salt into the bowl of a free-standing mixer fitted with a whisk attachment and whisk to soft peaks (you can also use an electric hand whisk). Add the cream of tartar then gradually whisk in the sugar until the mixture is stiff and glossy. Fold in the vanilla extract and the flour mixture and pour into the prepared tin.

Make a few holes in the mix with a skewer to let out the air bubbles and bake for 35–40 minutes until golden brown. Stand the mould on its feet. Meanwhile make the icing. Combine all the ingredients in a heatproof bowl and set over a pan of simmering water. Using an electric hand whisk, whisk the mixture until doubled in volume. Check the temperature of the mixture regularly with a sugar thermometer; once it reaches 70°C (160°F), remove from the heat and continue to whisk until stiff and glossy.

Cover the whole cake with the icing; it doesn't have to be neat as you're going to cover it with coconut. Pack the desiccated coconut over the cake then spoon in the berries.

NOTE: *If you can't find coconut extract, you can use vanilla extract instead.*

TIP: I use a block of ice cream so that I can shape it easily into a cylinder.

8

ARCTIC ROLL

When I was young this was my favourite pudding. I remember one New Year's Eve, I was going out with a boy and at midnight he took me out to his car where he'd laid out two bowls and spoons and an arctic roll because he knew how much I liked it! I remember thinking how lovely that was – in fact, so lovely that I also thought, 'He's being too nice', and I finished with him the next day. What a silly girl I was!

SERVES 8–10 (OR 2!)

butter, for greasing

1 litre (1¾ pints) vanilla ice cream

800 g (1 lb 12 oz) mixed berries

2 tablespoons icing sugar

3 large eggs

125 g (4½ oz) caster sugar, plus extra for rolling

60 g (2½ oz) plain flour

60 g (2½ oz) cornflour

1 teaspoon baking powder

METHOD: Preheat the oven to 180°C (350°F), gas mark 4, and grease and line a 35 x 25 cm (14 x 10 inch) Swiss roll tin with greaseproof paper.

Make a cylinder out of the ice cream by wrapping it in cling film and making a large sausage shape before refreezing until needed.

Put the berries and icing sugar into a saucepan and heat until you have a lovely, gooey compote. Leave to cool.

Tip the eggs and caster sugar into a bowl and use an electric whisk on a high setting to whisk until light and fluffy, about 6 minutes.

Mix together the flour, cornflour and baking powder, sift and fold into the egg mixture. Pour into the lined tin and bake for 12 minutes. The sponge should spring back when touched.

Sprinkle sugar on to a clean tea towel and lay the sponge on top. Peel off the greaseproof paper. Carefully roll the cake over from the long side, using the tea towel to guide you, and leave until ready to use.

To assemble, unroll the tea towel and spread a layer of compote on to the sponge. Take the ice cream cylinder from the freezer, unwrap and roll the ice cream up in the sponge. Refreeze for about an hour before serving.

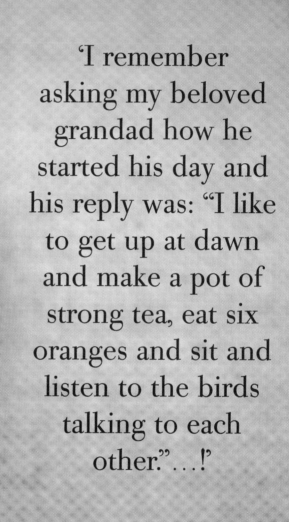

'I remember asking my beloved grandad how he started his day and his reply was: "I like to get up at dawn and make a pot of strong tea, eat six oranges and sit and listen to the birds talking to each other."…!'

9

POLENTA CAKE

✖

I have started using polenta a lot in my cooking. I love the texture and flavour it gives to this cake – it's dense and not too sweet. And the bright yellow colour is amazing!

SERVES 6–8

200 g (7 oz) unsalted butter, plus extra for greasing

200 g (7 oz) golden caster sugar

4 large eggs

200 g (7 oz) ground almonds

100 g (3½ oz) fine polenta

2 teaspoons baking powder

juice and zest of 1 lemon

2 tablespoons milk

METHOD: Preheat the oven to 180°C (350°F), gas mark 4, and grease and line a 23 cm (9 inch) springform cake tin with greaseproof paper.

In a large bowl, cream the butter and sugar until pale and fluffy, then beat in the eggs one at a time. Stir in the remaining ingredients.

Spoon the mixture into the lined tin and bake for 45–50 minutes until a skewer inserted into the centre of the cake comes out clean. Transfer to a wire rack to cool.

№ 10

CAKE IN A JAR

Last year I co-hosted a show called *What's Cooking?* – an hour of live cooking, chatting and fun. Because it was a live show, lots of things went wrong! Lovely chef Ben Ebbrell came on and made cake in a mug in a microwave. It was great fun, but we ended up blowing all the fuses in the studio by using two microwaves and the show fell off air! I really loved the idea, though, of making these quick and easy cakes. They don't look the prettiest once cooked, but they taste great (especially with a scoop of ice cream) and kids love to make them.

SERVES 2

4 tablespoons plain flour

2 tablespoons caster sugar

2 tablespoons cocoa powder

1 egg

3 tablespoons milk

3 tablespoons vegetable oil

¼ teaspoon vanilla (or peppermint) extract

METHOD: Put the flour, sugar and cocoa powder in a large jar and mix well. Add the egg and mix it in thoroughly to avoid any pockets of flour. Pour in the milk, oil and vanilla (or peppermint) extract and mix again.

Place in the microwave and cook for 3 minutes on maximum power (1000W). Wait until the cake stops rising and sets in the jar.

If necessary, run a knife around the sides of the cake and tip out of the jar while still warm on to a plate or saucer.

'I have a bit of a
collection of teapots
on the go – I just
can't resist them –
but my favourite is
an antique silver one.
I just love it and it
makes every tea time
a real treat!'

LISA

№ 11

PEANUT BUTTER CHEESECAKE

I am a big fan of cheesecake. I prefer the non-baked ones but, really, any will do! The thing I love about this one, though, is that it's not too sweet – you get an almost salty sweetness from the peanuts. The boys in my family go mad for this, so I serve big wedges with extra brittle on top!

SERVES 6–8

FOR THE BASE

50 g (2 oz) salted roasted peanuts
50 g (2 oz) caster sugar
200 g (7 oz) digestive biscuits
100 g (3½ oz) unsalted butter, melted

FOR THE FILLING

500 g (1 lb 2 oz) cream cheese
125 g (4½ oz) caster sugar
1 x 340 g (12 oz) jar smooth peanut butter
125 ml (4½ fl oz) sour cream
300 ml (½ pint) double cream

FOR THE STRAWBERRIES

250 g (9 oz) strawberries, hulled and halved
3 tablespoons icing sugar

FOR THE BRITTLE

150 g (5 oz) caster sugar
100 g (3½ oz) salted roasted peanuts

METHOD: Line a 23 cm (9 inch) springform cake tin with greaseproof paper. Tip the peanuts and sugar into a food processor and blitz until fine. Add the digestive biscuits and blitz until crushed. Tip into a bowl, stir through the melted butter then press into the base of the cake tin. Transfer to the fridge to set for around 30 minutes.

Meanwhile make the filling. Beat the cream cheese and sugar in a bowl until soft then beat in the peanut butter. Fold in the sour cream. Whisk the double cream to soft peaks then fold into the cheesecake mixture. Pour the filling on to the chilled biscuit base then return to the fridge for 4 hours, or overnight if possible.

While the cheesecake is setting, prepare the strawberries. Toss the halved strawberries with the icing sugar then set aside for 2 hours at room temperature. After 2 hours, drain the strawberries in a sieve set over a bowl. Pour the juices into a small pan and boil for 1 minute, until sticky, then pour over the strawberries and toss to coat. Refrigerate until needed.

To make the brittle, tip the sugar into a dry frying pan and melt it over a medium heat for 2–3 minutes. Don't stir, but swirl it around from time to time. Stir in the peanuts, making sure they are all covered in the caramel, then quickly tip them on to a baking tray lined with greaseproof paper or a silicone sheet. Leave to cool for 30 minutes, then break into shards.

Turn the cheesecake out on to a board, top with the strawberries and decorate with the brittle.

BIRTHDAY CAKES

My sister, Victoria, is the queen of birthday cakes. She has an amazing knack of turning a simple sponge or chocolate cake into something pretty spectacular! I have included a few of her photos here for inspiration. We are a family of girls with one boy, hence the number of girls' cakes! I hope you like them and they get your ideas flowing – it's amazing what a bit of glitter icing can do, and you can buy so many cake decorations and little figures on the internet, there really is no limit to your imagination.

I think the key with children's birthday cakes is to remember they are just that. So keep them fun, and know that the cake is there to be eaten. Make them delicious and ice them whatever way you like – it's not a competition and most children will just love anything sweet and sticky!

A FEW IDEAS TO INSPIRE YOU

Get yourself a large rectangular cake tin and your options are endless!

- Ice the cake in green and mark out a football pitch – this is a sure hit with boys of all ages! You can buy the little football figures and goals online, although most larger cake decorating shops will sell them. You can even buy the pitch ready made and lay it on top if you don't want to ice the whole cake yourself.

- It doesn't have to be a football, of course – if you have a fan of rugby, cricket, tennis, baseball – even swimming! – just ice the cake and add little players and fans across the top!

- Pirate chest – ice the cake in brown and cut out a cardboard treasure chest lid. Cover the lid in icing and wedge it into the back of the cake. Then cover the cake with gold coins, candy necklaces and those tiny silver sugar balls for a pirate's haul!

- Shark attack – cover the cake in blue and use blue piping icing to create waves, then top them with flecks of white icing – like sea spray. Sprinkle with glitter and decorate with figures – don't forget the shark!

- Jewellery box – use the same method as for the pirate chest but cover the cake in jelly gems and rings instead.

№ 12

PRINCESS BIRTHDAY CAKE

My godmother Nina made a beautiful princess cake for my niece Lola's eighth birthday. I was super-impressed – a brilliant birthday cake for a little girl! The cake forms the skirt of the princess! You will need a princess doll to sit on top.

SERVES ABOUT 20 CHILDREN

225 g (8 oz) butter, softened, plus extra for greasing
225 g (8 oz) caster sugar
4 eggs
225 g (8 oz) self-raising flour
1 teaspoon vanilla extract
1 tablespoon milk

FOR THE BUTTER ICING

375 g (13 oz) icing sugar
125 g (4½ oz) butter
1 tablespoon milk

TO DECORATE

few drops of pink food colouring
1 kg (2 lb 3 oz) packet ready-to-roll icing

METHOD: Preheat the oven to 180°C (350°F), gas mark 4, and grease and line a 2 litre (3½ pint) pudding basin with greaseproof paper.

Cream the butter and sugar together until pale and fluffy. Add the eggs, one at a time, and fold in the flour, vanilla extract and milk. Pour into the prepared basin and cook for about 40 minutes until the sponge springs back when you press it lightly with your fingertips.

Meanwhile make the butter icing by beating all the ingredients together in a bowl.

Turn the sponge out on to a wire rack to cool. When cooled, place on a cake board and cut in half horizontally. Sandwich the two halves with a layer of butter icing then cover the whole cake with the remaining butter icing.

Add a few drops of pink food colouring (depending on how bright you want the colour to be) to the icing and knead until smooth. Roll out and lay over the cake – it can sit in folds like material and be tucked underneath. Cut a hole to poke the princess through the top.

Decorate the cake however you like – edible silver balls and flower decorations are always fun.

№ 13

RED VELVET CUPCAKES

My first memory of red velvet cupcakes is a beautiful, crisp spring day in New York. Walking along, I saw this pretty cake in a bakery and just had to try one. It was light as a feather and deep with flavour, and the frosting on top just brought it all together. I'm not usually one for icing and, to my family's annoyance, I usually scrape it off. However, I ate every single bit of this cake!

MAKES 24

125 g (4½ oz) unsalted butter, softened
300 g (10½ oz) golden caster sugar
3 large eggs
180 g (6 oz) plain flour
2 tablespoons cocoa powder
½ teaspoon fine salt
125 ml (4½ fl oz) buttermilk
1 teaspoon Superflair red food colouring
1 teaspoon vanilla extract
1 teaspoon bicarbonate of soda
2 teaspoons red wine vinegar

FOR THE ICING

150 g (5 oz) white chocolate
200 g (7 oz) cream cheese
100 g (3½ oz) unsalted butter, softened
200 g (7 oz) icing sugar
1 teaspoon vanilla extract

METHOD: Preheat the oven to 170°C (325°F), gas mark 3, and line two 12-hole cupcake trays with paper cases.

Cream the butter and sugar together until pale and fluffy, then beat in the eggs one at a time. Sift the flour, cocoa powder and salt into a bowl then gradually fold into the batter.

Combine the buttermilk, food colouring and vanilla and fold into the batter. In a separate bowl, mix together the bicarbonate of soda and vinegar and carefully fold into the batter, taking care to keep as much air in the mixture as possible. Divide between the paper cases and bake for 20 minutes, until a skewer inserted into the centre of a cupcake comes out clean. Transfer to a wire rack to cool.

Meanwhile, melt the chocolate in a heatproof bowl set over a pan of gently simmering water then set aside to cool for a couple of minutes. Beat the cream cheese and butter until smooth then beat in the white chocolate, icing sugar and vanilla. Cover and refrigerate for 1 hour before using.

Continued overleaf

When the cupcakes have cooled, trim the tops slightly. Blitz the trimmings in a food processor until they resemble breadcrumbs and set aside. Spoon or pipe the icing on to the cupcakes and sprinkle with the red velvet crumbs.

TIP: Try not to use too much food colouring – you don't want to be able to taste it.

№ 14

STRAWBERRY MILKCAKE

If you are a fan of strawberry milkshake, then this is the cake for you! I think it makes a fab birthday cake too, decorated with fresh strawberries. The pink milkshake icing tastes so much of my childhood that if I close my eyes and take a great big bite I might as well be back in junior school!

SERVES 6–8

300 g (10½ oz) butter, softened, plus extra for greasing

300 g (10½ oz) Nesquik strawberry milk powder

4 eggs

300 g (10½ oz) self-raising flour

4 tablespoons milk

a little pink or red food colouring

FOR THE ICING

300 g (10½ oz) butter, softened

500 g (1 lb 2 oz) icing sugar

pink or red food colouring

150 g (5 oz) Nesquik strawberry milk powder

50 ml (2 fl oz) milk

METHOD: Preheat the oven to 180°C (350°F), gas mark 4, and grease and line two 20 cm (8 inch) cake tins with greaseproof paper.

Cream the butter and strawberry milk powder together until pink and fluffy. Add the eggs one by one, alternating with a spoonful of flour, then add the remaining flour, milk and as much pink or red food colouring as you need to create a delicious pink batter.

Divide the mixture between the cake tins and bake in the preheated oven for 30–40 minutes, until a skewer inserted into the centre comes away clean. Cool in the tin for 10 minutes then turn out on to a wire rack to cool completely.

To make the icing, cream the butter and icing sugar together with an electric hand whisk until light and fluffy, then add enough colouring to turn it pink. Mix the strawberry milk powder with the milk and add to the icing. There should be enough to sandwich the cakes together and cover the outside!

'I really think making
cakes should be fun – it's
not about perfection, it's
about how *you* like it!'

LISA

№ 15

CHERRY FINANCIERS

I made these a lot, nearly every week when I worked at a restaurant. They are served as petits fours along with pâte de fruits and chocolates. I love them with a cup of tea, just out of the oven. You can use whatever fruit you want but I especially like cherries or blueberries. I also like to use salted butter for a bit of a savoury note, but you can use unsalted if you prefer.

MAKES 35–40

185 g (6½ oz) butter
200 g (7 oz) icing sugar
90 g (3¼ oz) plain flour
100 g (3½ oz) ground almonds

6 egg whites
blueberries, fresh pitted cherries or maraschino cherries
icing sugar, for dusting (optional)

METHOD: Preheat the oven to 180°C (350°F), gas mark 4.

Melt the butter in a saucepan over a low heat. Once it has melted, leave it on the heat until a nice brown sediment forms and it starts to smell nutty – this is *beurre noisette*, or brown butter.

Mix together the icing sugar, flour and ground almonds. In a separate bowl, whisk the egg whites until frothy, then whisk in the dry ingredients. Whisk this mixture into the *beurre noisette*.

Pour the mixture into a piping bag and allow to rest in the fridge for an hour before piping into tiny muffin moulds, about three-quarters full (they will puff up as they cook).

Push a cherry or a blueberry into the centre of each mould and bake in the oven for about 12–15 minutes. Leave to cool in their moulds and then carefully turn out. Dust with a little icing sugar if you fancy.

NOTE: You can buy silicone financier moulds, or simply use tiny muffin moulds.

4

CHOCOLATE

CHOCOLATE!

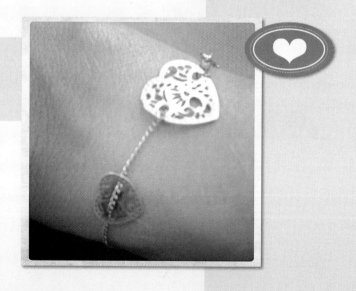

What is it about chocolate? Sometimes it's all I want. There are days when everything feels like an uphill struggle, and I love nothing more than when the day is done and I can finally sit down on the sofa with a cup of tea and something sweet and chocolatey – chocolate cake, chocolate tart, chocolate spread… the list goes on! This chapter is dedicated to all things chocolate!

№ 1

STICKY CHOCOLATE LOAF CAKE

✄

This is a really gooey, soft chocolate cake that will go some way to solving all life's problems. Add a pinch of salt to the melted chocolate – for a slightly salty icing.

MAKES I LOAF

250 g (9 oz) unsalted butter, softened,
    plus extra for greasing

225 g (8 oz) muscovado sugar

3 eggs

150 g (5 oz) golden syrup

1 tablespoon vanilla bean paste

100 g (3½ oz) dark chocolate, melted

225 g (8 oz) plain flour

25 g (1 oz) good quality cocoa powder

1 teaspoon bicarbonate of soda

250 ml (9 fl oz) boiling water

FOR THE ICING

125 ml (4½ fl oz) water

50 g (2 oz) cocoa powder

150 g (5 oz) golden syrup

100 g (3½ oz) dark chocolate, chopped

25 g (1 oz) butter

METHOD: Preheat the oven to 190°C (375°F), gas mark 5, and place a loaf paper into a 900 g (2 lb) loaf tin, or grease and line with greaseproof paper.

Place the butter in a large bowl or in the bowl of a stand mixer. Add the sugar and beat until really light and fluffy. Add the eggs, one at a time, beating well between each addition. Slowly add the golden syrup, vanilla bean paste and melted chocolate.

Sift the flour, cocoa powder and bicarbonate of soda together. Add one third of the dry mixture to the bowl and beat in then add half the water. Add another third of the dry mixture followed by the remaining water and finally the rest of the dry mixture.

Pour the mixture carefully into the loaf tin and bake for 30 minutes. Reduce the oven to 170°C (325°F), gas mark 3, and bake for a further 30–40 minutes until a skewer inserted into the centre comes out almost clean. Remove from the oven and allow to cool in the tin.

To make the chocolate topping, put the water, cocoa powder and syrup in a small saucepan. Whisk together and bring to the boil. Simmer for 3 minutes then remove from the heat and beat in the chocolate and butter. Spread over the top of the cake.

№ 2

SELF-SAUCING
CHOCOLATE PUDDING

⁜

This recipe is genius. It is so easy and is one of the most delicious things in this book. All you have to do is mix up the pudding and set it in the fridge a day in advance. Then, just before you put it in the oven, sprinkle sugar and cocoa powder on top and pour over some boiling water. When the pudding comes out it will be sitting in its own sticky chocolate sauce, which you can spoon back over the top.

SERVES 4–6

125 g (4½ oz) plain flour

pinch of salt

60 g (2½ oz) caster sugar

2 teaspoons baking powder

2 tablespoons cocoa powder

120 ml (4 fl oz) milk

40 g (1½ oz) butter, melted

1 egg

1–2 drops of vanilla extract

FOR THE TOPPING

180 g (6 oz) muscovado sugar

2 tablespoons cocoa powder

250 ml (9 fl oz) boiling water

METHOD: Sift the flour, salt, caster sugar, baking powder and cocoa powder into a bowl.

Combine the milk, butter, egg and vanilla extract in another bowl, then mix the wet and dry ingredients together.

Pour the mixture into a 1 litre (2 pint) pie dish. Cover with cling film and put in the fridge overnight to set.

THE NEXT DAY...

Preheat the oven to 180°C (350°F), gas mark 4. Sprinkle the muscovado sugar and cocoa powder over the pudding and pour the boiling water over the top. Bake in the preheated oven for 45 minutes, until the pudding is puffy and firm in the centre.

Remove from the oven and serve with pouring cream or ice cream.

№ 3

ANN'S CHOCOLATE BROWNIES

My godmother Ann is a fantastic cook and her brownies are legendary. In fact, they are held in such high regard that wherever and whenever we eat brownies that aren't hers, the comment is usually, 'Not as good as Ann's!' These brownies are the perfect combination of crispy and chewy. They are best eaten when they've been out of the oven for about an hour but are still warm and gooey. For extra indulgence – or if your day has been particularly fraught – serve with a scoop of vanilla ice cream.

MAKES 32

125 g (4½ oz) dark chocolate
150 g (5 oz) butter, plus extra for greasing
4 eggs
500 g (1 lb 2 oz) caster sugar
175 g (6 oz) plain flour
1 teaspoon baking powder
1 teaspoon salt

METHOD: Preheat the oven to 180°C (350°F), gas mark 4, and grease two 20 cm (8 inch) square tins.

Grate the chocolate into the butter and melt in saucepan over a low heat until combined.

Whisk the eggs and sugar together until pale and then stir in the melted chocolate.

Sift the flour, baking powder and salt into the mix and fold in. Pour the mixture into the tins and bake for about 30 minutes, until the top has a nice crust but the brownies are still gooey inside.

Leave in the tins to cool completely before cutting into 5 cm (2 inch) squares. These will keep for up to 1 week in an airtight container.

№ 4

MUMMY'S SALTED CHOCOLATE CAKE

✳

This recipe was also in my first book but I make it so often that I couldn't not have it here as well. It is easy peasy and something my mum used to whip up in a heartbeat. The combination of salt and chocolate is one of my favourite things, but if you don't like it feel free to leave out the salt.

SERVES 8–10

FOR THE CAKE

175 g (6 oz) unsalted butter, softened, plus extra for greasing

175 g (6 oz) caster sugar

3 large eggs

175 g (6 oz) self-raising flour

1½ teaspoons baking powder

2 tablespoons drinking chocolate

1 tablespoon warm water

FOR THE FILLING

125 g (4½ oz) icing sugar

40 g (1½ oz) unsalted butter, softened

1 tablespoon whole milk

FOR THE ICING

225 g (8 oz) dark chocolate, broken into pieces and melted

100 g (3½ oz) unsalted butter

125 ml (4½ fl oz) double cream

½ teaspoon sea salt

METHOD: Preheat the oven to 180°C (350°F), gas mark 4, and grease one or two 20 cm (8 inch) cake tins.

Cream the butter and sugar together then whisk in the eggs. Fold in the flour, baking powder and drinking chocolate, then stir in the warm water. Pour into the cake tin or tins. Bake in the oven for 20 minutes (check on it after 15 minutes), or until the cake springs back when pressed lightly with your finger. Turn out on to a rack and leave to cool. When cool, cut in half carefully if using one cake tin, and prepare the filling.

Mix all the filling ingredients together. Spread on one half of the cake and sandwich together with the other half.

To make the icing, mix the melted chocolate and butter together with the double cream and salt, and spread on top of the cake. Simple!

№ 5

NATALIE'S CHOCOLATE & FENNEL POTS

The winner of 2013's *MasterChef* was the brilliant Natalie Coleman. I was so excited that she won and got to cook with her the day after the final aired. Natalie was nervous because it was her first time on live TV (although she didn't need to be!) and she held my hand under the counter until it was time to cook. I loved her for that and we became friends. We've cooked together many times since then at the BBC Good Food Shows and she is great fun as well as a super-talented cook. The chocolate and fennel were components of one of Natalie's dishes that I thought was a delicious stand-alone dessert, so I asked her if I could include it.

MAKES 4–6

200 ml (7 fl oz) double cream
200 g (7 oz) dark chocolate
(minimum 70% cocoa solids),
broken into pieces

1 tablespoon Pernod
pinch of fennel pollen

METHOD: Heat the double cream in a saucepan until nearly boiling then remove from the heat.

Place the chocolate in a heatproof bowl over a pan of simmering water (do not let the water touch the bowl). Melt the chocolate then remove from the heat and stir in the warm cream and Pernod.

Divide between 4–6 individual pots or glasses before leaving to set in the fridge for at least 1 hour. Sprinkle over the fennel pollen just before serving.

№ 6

CHOCOLATE ÉCLAIRS

I have yet to meet someone who doesn't like a chocolate éclair! When my sister and I were little we used to love these. I loved the pastry and the custard inside, but sometimes I wanted just a bit of the chocolate so I would peel or scrape most of my chocolate from the top and give the rest to Victoria. We would make a right mess, mouths and faces covered in squishy custard and chocolate but, boy, were they good! The choux pastry is a basic in my book. It is light and crisp and easy to master, so have fun with it.

MAKES 20

FOR THE CHOUX PASTRY
90 g (3¼ oz) butter
360 ml (12½ fl oz) water
pinch each of salt and sugar
110 g (4 oz) plain flour, sifted
3 whole eggs, beaten well

FOR THE FILLING
200 ml (7 fl oz) custard (see page 192)
2 tablespoons icing sugar

1 vanilla pod, split and seeds
    scraped out

FOR THE ICING
100 g (3½ oz) dark chocolate, broken
    into pieces
40 g (1½ oz) unsalted butter
80 g (3 oz) icing sugar, sifted
1–2 tablespoons water

METHOD: Preheat the oven to 200°C (400°F), gas mark 6. To make the pastry, put the butter and water in a medium saucepan, add the salt and sugar, and bring to the boil. Make sure the butter is melted.

Remove from the heat, add the sifted flour all at once and really beat it in with a wooden spoon until the mixture comes away from the sides of the pan. Return to the heat and cook for 2 minutes until the paste is pale. Cool a little.

Add the beaten eggs, a little at a time, incorporating fully with a wooden spoon after each addition. The mixture will go glossy then back to dull. Add the eggs until the mixture is shiny and it JUST drops off the wooden spoon. Cool the mixture for about 10 minutes before transferring to a piping bag fitted with a 1 cm (½ inch) plain nozzle.

Pipe 10 cm (4 inch) lengths on to two baking sheets lined with greaseproof paper, leaving plenty of space between each one.

Continued overleaf

⋇

Bake for 15–20 minutes, then turn down the oven to 160°C (320°), gas mark 2, and bake for a further 15 minutes, until golden. Transfer to a wire rack to cool to room temperature.

Meanwhile, make the filling. Whisk the custard, icing sugar and vanilla seeds to soft peaks.

For the icing, put the chocolate into a heatproof bowl set over a pan of simmering water (make sure the bowl does not touch the water). Stir until the chocolate has completely melted then remove the bowl from the pan. Beat in the butter and icing sugar until smooth then gradually beat in the water, a little at a time, until you have a smooth, glossy icing.

When the éclairs are completely cool, pierce the bases and pipe the vanilla custard inside.

Dip the top of each éclair into the icing and wipe off any excess. Leave the finished éclairs to set for 10 minutes before serving.

TARTE DE ST EMILION
AU CHOCOLAT

✳

I made this rich chocolate tart over Christmas and my lovely friend Dan ended up taking the last pieces home for his tea. You only need a sliver and it's gorgeous served with crème fraîche.

SERVES 8–10

FOR THE PASTRY
200 g (7 oz) plain flour
good pinch of salt
50 g (2 oz) ground almonds
120 g (4 oz) cold butter, diced
1 egg, separated

FOR THE FILLING
250 g (9 oz) plain chocolate
250 ml (9 fl oz) double cream
2 eggs, separated
80 g (3 oz) golden caster sugar
1 tablespoon Amaretto (optional)
handful of crushed amaretti biscuits

METHOD: Mix together the flour, salt and ground almonds in a food processor, then add the butter and pulse until the mixture resembles breadcrumbs. Add the egg yolk and about 2 tablespoons of cold water and pulse again until the mixture just comes together. Flatten into a disc, cover in cling film and leave to rest in the fridge for at least 30 minutes.

Preheat the oven to 180°C (350°F), gas mark 4. Roll the pastry out to the thickness of a pound coin and line a 23 cm (9 inch) tart tin. I always leave quite a large overhang. Bake for 20 minutes. Leave to cool then trim off the excess pastry with a serrated knife. For a really crispy case, brush with egg white and put back in the oven for 5 minutes. Leave to cool. Reduce the oven temperature to 150°C (300°F), gas mark 2.

Melt the chocolate in a bowl over a pan of simmering water (make sure the bottom of the bowl doesn't actually touch the hot water). Add the cream and stir well. Set aside.

In a separate bowl whisk the egg whites to soft peaks then add 30 g (1 oz) of the sugar and whisk again until you have a glossy meringue that's not too stiff.

In another bowl whisk the egg yolks and the rest of the sugar until thick. Mix the chocolate mix into the egg yolks. Add the Amaretto, if using. Finally, fold in the egg whites.

Pour the filling into the tart case, sprinkle the crushed amaretti biscuits over the top and bake for 15 minutes. The tart should still have a little wobble.

№ 8

CHOCOLATE AFTER-DINNER MINT BISCUITS

These are great any time of day… not just after dinner!

MAKES 15

250 g (9 oz) plain flour
150 g (5 oz) icing sugar
50 g (2 oz) cocoa powder
pinch of salt
225 g (8 oz) cold butter, cubed
1 egg yolk

FOR THE FILLING

180 g (6¼ oz) dark chocolate
160 ml (5½ fl oz) double cream
2–4 drops of peppermint extract

METHOD: Sift the flour, icing sugar and cocoa powder into a food processor. Add a pinch of salt and the butter and pulse until the mixture resembles breadcrumbs. Add the egg yolk and pulse again until the mixture comes together. Turn out on to a work surface and knead very gently to form a dough. Roll into a cylinder 5 cm (2 inches) in diameter, wrap in cling film and refrigerate for about 30 minutes until firm.

Preheat the oven to 180°C (350°F), gas mark 4, and line a baking tray with greaseproof paper.

Cut the dough into 5 mm (¼ inch) slices and arrange on the baking tray. Bake in the preheated oven for 10–12 minutes. Allow to cool slightly on the tray before transferring the biscuits to a wire rack.

To make the filling, break the chocolate into very small pieces and set aside in a bowl. In a saucepan heat the cream until simmering then stir into the chocolate until smooth. Add a few drops of peppermint extract to taste and leave to cool.

Spread a little of the filling onto the biscuits and sandwich together.

№ 9

CHOC SPREAD

✄

I love Nutella but I also like plain chocolate spread. Why mess with genius, you may ask? Nutella is ace! You're right, but sometimes it's nice to make your own jar of gooey rich chocolate spread, and this is perfect for those who can't eat nuts. It will keep in the fridge for about a month.

MAKES 650 G (1 LB 6 OZ)

100 g (3½ oz) milk chocolate
100 g (3½ oz) dark chocolate
4 tablespoons vegetable oil

pinch of salt
1 x 397 g (14 oz) tin condensed milk

METHOD: Melt both the chocolates with the oil and salt in a heatproof bowl set over a pan of simmering water – don't let the bowl actually touch the hot water. Remove from the heat.

Mix in the condensed milk and 3 tablespoons of hot water from the saucepan, then transfer to a stand mixer and whip on a medium-low setting for about 5–10 minutes until cool. It should have the consistency of a cake mixture with bubbles in. Pour into a jar and refrigerate overnight.

5

TEATIME

TIME
FOR
TEA!

Just as I remember the summers when I was growing up as endless days of sunshine, freshly cut grass and water sprinklers, my teatimes were made up of mini sandwiches, buttery crumpets and hot toasted teacakes – and my Auntie Elsie's famous trifle! I like to think we did those things all the time, but just as those idyllic summer days probably only happened a few times a year, in reality a teatime like that would only be for special occasions. I think that's what has made the memories all the more magnificent. Whether you're having a party or just the family over for Sunday afternoon, this chapter includes a little bit of savoury, a lot of sweet and a nod to those childhood fantasies! ✳

№ 1

LISA'S PERFECT CUP OF TEA

'Nothing makes me happier than a cup of Earl Grey tea. Tea just makes everything seem alright again. I love all sorts of tea, from good old builders' to green tea to jasmine tea and most things in between. But for me, a pot of Earl Grey and a big china cup and the world seems a happier place. I'm not sure if it's the ritual of making tea, the comforting feeling of holding the cup in your hands or those precious ten minutes that allow you to sit, to think, to daydream. . . to take a deep breath.

Tea holds a place in some of my earliest memories too. My grandma Betty lived by the sea and my sister and I used to go and stay with her in the holidays. Betty used to have a Teasmade and every morning at 7am the alarm would go off and I'd lie in bed in the spare room listening to the really loud gurgle of hot water and steam, followed by the clinking of cups being laid out and of tea being poured into them. Betty had slightly shaky hands and the sound of the cup and saucer wobbling into the bedroom, and then the curtains being thrown open filled me with all that hope and excitement of a new day. Now, nearly every morning I wake up early and sit in bed or on my sofa looking out at my garden, thinking about the day ahead, and always with a cup of tea.'

№ 2

MILK LOAF

�

I think tea as I recall it as a child has fizzled out a bit. I remember milk loaf and biscuits, and boiled eggs and soldiers… Maybe it was because we used to have a hot lunch and then a long wait until my dad got home from work for dinner, so in between we would have tea. I'm not sure; perhaps it was just on weekends when my parents were having dinner parties. Whatever the case, we loved teatime!

MAKES I LOAF

500 g (1 lb 2 oz) strong white bread
   flour, plus extra for dusting
1 teaspoon salt
300 ml (½ pint) lukewarm Jersey milk

2 x 7 g (¼ oz) sachets fast-action
   dried yeast
50 g (2 oz) butter, melted
1 teaspoon sugar
olive oil, for greasing

METHOD: Tip the flour and salt into a large bowl and make a well in the centre. Combine the milk, yeast, butter and sugar in a jug and stir until the sugar has dissolved. Pour the liquid into the well in the centre of the flour. Using a fork, stir the mixture until it forms a rough dough, then use your hands to bring everything together.

Dust a clean work surface with flour and tip out the dough. Knead for a good 10 minutes until smooth and elastic. To knead, use the heel of your hand to stretch the dough away from you, then pull back into a ball. Turn the dough through 90 degrees then repeat. The more you work the dough at this stage, the lighter the finished loaf will be. Alternatively, combine the ingredients in a free-standing mixer fitted with a dough hook and knead for 3 minutes on the slowest speed, then 6 minutes on the second slowest speed.

Transfer the dough to a lightly oiled bowl and dust the top with flour. Cover with a clean tea towel or a sheet of cling film and leave to rise in a warm place for 2 hours until doubled in size.

Remove the tea towel and punch the dough once to knock out the air. Grease the milk loaf tin with a little oil and dust with flour. Shape the dough into a rough oblong and lay in the tin. Close the tin and leave to rise in a warm place for 1 hour.

Preheat the oven to 200°C (400°F), gas mark 6. Bake for 35–40 minutes then leave to cool for 5 minutes in the tin. Turn out on to a wire rack and leave to cool before slicing.

NOTE: You will need a special milk loaf tin to get the classic cylinder shape, but you can also just make this in a regular 900 g (2 lb) loaf tin.

NOTE:

These recipes make enough for a tea party;
I don't really need to tell you that you can
scale them up and down depending on how
many you may need . . .

№ 3

FINGER SANDWICHES

✕

When I go out to tea (which is not often enough in my opinion!) I love the sandwiches. I know it's like teaching you the ABC but here are my two favourite fillings – a little bit of mint added to the cucumber makes them really fresh, and the salmon mousse is just delish!

SMOKED SALMON, CREAM CHEESE & CHIVE MOUSSE

MAKES 24 FINGER SANDWICHES

1 tablespoon soft butter

100 ml (3½ fl oz) double cream

200 g (7 oz) smoked salmon

1 tablespoon cream cheese

juice of ½ lemon

1 tablespoon chopped chives

black pepper

16 slices of bread

METHOD: Blend the butter, cream and salmon in a food processor until smooth. Scrape into a bowl and then beat in the cream cheese, lemon juice and chopped chives. Season with pepper (you don't need any salt, as the salmon will be salty enough). Chill in the fridge.

Spread half the slices of bread generously with the salmon mixture and then top with the remaining bread. Press down lightly then trim off the crusts. Cut each sandwich into three strips.

TIP: Sometimes I like to toast them. Before slicing them into fingers, fry them on each side, including the edges, in lots of butter until lightly golden.

CUCUMBER & MINT

MAKES 24 FINGER SANDWICHES

1 cucumber

small bunch of fresh mint

butter, for spreading

16 slices of bread

METHOD: Peel the cucumber and then very finely slice it – you want the cucumber slices to be almost wafer thin.

Butter all the bread. Top half the slices with overlapping layers of cucumber. Scatter over a few mint leaves then top with the remaining bread. Trim off the crusts and cut into fingers.

№ 4

FRIED GOAT'S
CHEESE SANDWICHES

✳

This really is just a posh version of a toasted sandwich, but I like to make even the simplest things look pretty. Maybe I have too much time on my hands…!!

MAKES 4

8 slices white bread, crusts removed

4 thin slices from a large goat's
   cheese log

4 slices Serrano ham

2 ripe figs, sliced

2 tablespoons olive oil

½ teaspoon sea salt

METHOD: Roll out each slice of bread with a rolling pin to half its original thickness.

Using a knife or a cutter, cut out a circle from each piece of bread in the shape of the cheese. Place a slice of goat's cheese on a bread circle, add a slice of Serrano ham and half a fig. Top with another circle of bread and press down. Repeat for the other three sandwiches.

Heat 1 tablespoon of the olive oil in a non-stick frying pan and fry the sandwiches for 2 minutes on each side until golden brown and crisp. You may need to do this in batches and top up the olive oil as necessary.

№ 5

MINI CORONATION CHICKEN TARTLETS

✤

These are very similar to vol-au-vents and with the Coronation chicken filling they're like tiny little mouthfuls of the '70s! Make double because they go in seconds!

MAKES 24

butter, for greasing

320 g (11 oz) ready-rolled all-butter puff pastry

FOR THE CORONATION CHICKEN FILLING

1 teaspoon butter

2 spring onions, finely sliced

large pinch of curry powder (about ¼ teaspoon)

2 tablespoons finely chopped dried apricots

1 teaspoon tomato purée

2 tablespoons double cream

2 tablespoons mayonnaise

1 teaspoon Greek yogurt

200 g (7 oz) cooked chicken breasts, finely chopped

salt and freshly ground black pepper

TO SERVE

cucumber slices

METHOD: Preheat the oven to 220°C (425°F), gas mark 7, and grease two 12-hole mini muffin trays with butter.

Roll out the puff pastry to make it a little thinner then cut out 24 circles of pastry, each 6 cm (2½ inches) in diameter, and use them to line the muffin trays. Prick the bases of the tartlets with a fork (so they don't puff up as much when they cook) and then bake in the oven for 20 minutes. Remove from the oven and leave to cool. (If your tartlets have puffed up a lot anyway, just remove the top layer of pastry to reveal the hollow underneath.)

Meanwhile, melt the butter in a small pan and fry the spring onions until soft. Stir in the curry powder and cook for 1 minute.

Remove from the heat, add the chopped apricots and tomato purée and combine well.

Leave to cool, then stir in the cream, mayonnaise and yogurt. Stir the chicken into the sauce to coat evenly then season to taste with salt and pepper.

Spoon a teaspoonful of the chicken mixture into each pastry case and serve with cucumber slices.

PANCETTA & RICOTTA
'TARTS'

✳

I'm always on the lookout for a new breakfast idea so I was delighted to discover these tasty 'tarts'. Having said that, serving them at teatime, piled on a pretty plate, makes me very happy, too! They are simple and really effective – oh, and you'll eat the whole plate…

MAKES 8

8–10 slices pancetta
500 g (1 lb 2 oz) ricotta cheese
125 g (4½ oz) Gruyère cheese, grated

1 egg
salt and freshly ground black pepper

METHOD: Preheat the oven to 180°C (350°F), gas mark 4.

Lightly grease 8 muffin cups and line each one with a pancetta slice – cut a little off another strip of pancetta, if necessary.

Put the ricotta, Gruyère, egg, salt and pepper into a bowl and mix together.

Spoon the mixture into the prepared muffin tins and press down to flatten.

Bake for about 25 minutes until the 'tarts' are set.

№ 7

LEEK & LANCASHIRE CHEESE BREAD & BUTTER PUDDINGS

These mini loaves of savoury bread and butter pudding make a fabulous teatime treat. They are very easy and are great served hot or cold.

MAKES 8

25 g (1 oz) salted butter,
    plus extra for greasing
2 small leeks, finely sliced
1 egg plus 2 egg yolks
2 teaspoons mustard powder
150 ml (¼ pint) double cream
150 ml (¼ pint) whole milk
50 g (2 oz) Lancashire cheese,
    grated

2 teaspoons finely chopped chives,
    plus extra to serve
5 slices stale white bread
sea salt and freshly ground black
    pepper

TO SERVE
2 slices smoked streaky bacon

METHOD: Preheat the oven to 180°C (350°F), gas mark 4, and grease eight 5 x 8 cm (2 x 3¼ inch) miniature loaf tins.

Heat the butter in a frying pan until foaming then add the leeks and fry gently for 10 minutes until soft and caramelised. Remove from the heat and leave to cool.

Whisk together the egg, egg yolks, mustard powder, cream and milk until smooth. Stir in the cooled leeks, cheese and chives, and season with salt and pepper. Using the bottom of one of the loaf tins as a guide, cut out 8 rectangles of bread. Dip them in the egg mixture then lay in the bottom of each tin. Cut the remaining bread into 1 cm (½ inch) cubes and stir through the egg mixture. Divide the mixture between the tins, place on a baking tray and bake for 15 minutes until risen and golden brown. Remove from the oven and leave to cool slightly.

Meanwhile, fry the bacon in a dry non-stick pan for 2–3 minutes on each side until crisp then drain on kitchen paper. Leave to cool then finely slice. Serve the bread and butter puddings sprinkled with the bacon and chives.

'I have a bit of a spoon fetish! I'm constantly picking them up when I see them in junk shops.'

№ 8

STILTON GOUGÈRES

One of the most exciting places I went to eat last year was a restaurant in Paris called Le Chateaubriand. We sat at the bar and the dishes started arriving, one delicious and amazing plate after another. The next morning I wrote it all down – I never want to forget that night! The first dish was a tiny plate of gougères – which are really just like savoury profiteroles – and I promised myself that when I got home I would learn how to make them.

MAKES 35–40

250 ml (9 fl oz) water
100 g (3½ oz) salted butter
pinch of caster sugar
150 g (5 oz) plain flour
4 large eggs, beaten
200 g (7 oz) Stilton, crumbled
freshly ground white pepper
sea salt flakes

METHOD: Preheat the oven to 220°C (425°F), gas mark 7, and line two baking sheets with greaseproof paper.

Bring the water, butter and sugar to the boil in a saucepan then whisk in the flour. Reduce the heat slightly and continue to cook for 2–3 minutes until the mixture starts to pull away from the sides of the pan and form a smooth ball.

Tip the mixture into the bowl of a free-standing mixer fitted with a paddle attachment and beat for 1 minute until cooled slightly. With the motor running, gradually add the beaten eggs until fully incorporated. Continue to beat for a further 1–2 minutes until the mixture is smooth and silky. Beat in the Stilton (don't worry about any small lumps) and season with white pepper.

Using a rubber spatula, transfer the mixture to a large piping bag fitted with a 1 cm (½ inch) plain round nozzle. Chill for 1 hour. Pipe tablespoon-sized balls of the mixture on to the prepared baking sheets, leaving a 4–5 cm (2 inch) gap between each – they will spread during cooking. Bake for 10 minutes then reduce the heat to 180°C (350°F), gas mark 4, and bake for a further 20 minutes until golden. Remove from the oven, sprinkle with salt and serve warm.

№ 9

CHEESE SCONES

✳

These are perfect on those cold drizzly afternoons when the last thing you really want to do is take the kids out to the park, but they need a run around and you need your sanity! Coming home and eating these warm from the oven with melted butter and a grind of black pepper (for me) or jam (for Billie) makes you feel like all is well with the world!

MAKES ABOUT 6–8

225 g (8 oz) self-raising flour

pinch of salt

½ teaspoon mustard powder

½ teaspoon cayenne pepper

55 g (2 oz) butter, diced

25 g (1 oz) Comté cheese (or any other mature hard cheese), finely grated

125–150 ml (4–5 fl oz) milk, plus a little extra for brushing

---

METHOD: Preheat the oven to 220°C (425°F), gas mark 7, and line a baking tray with silicone or baking paper.

Sift the dry ingredients into a bowl. Add the butter and rub in until the mixture resembles breadcrumbs. Mix through the grated cheese. Add the milk gradually to bring the mixture together as dough.

On a floured surface, knead lightly and pat the dough out into a 2 cm (¾ inch) thick round. Using a 5 cm (2 inch) cutter, stamp out the scones and place on the baking sheet, re-kneading the leftovers to make more.

Brush the tops of the scones with milk and bake in the oven for about 12–15 minutes, until golden. Cool on a wire rack.

TIP: My great-grandmother, 'Nannie', used to make these scones for us. She used wholemeal flour, but I prefer white flour.

№ 10

CRUMPETS

✕

Sunday roast, autumn walks, open fires, hot chocolate and crumpets for tea in our pyjamas… these are the memories that make Sundays seem OK. In reality, they probably only happened a few times but that makes the memories all the more precious.

MAKES 8

330 ml (11 fl oz) milk

1 teaspoon caster sugar

225 g (8 oz) plain flour

1 teaspoon fine salt

2 x 7 g (¼ oz) sachets fast-action
    dried yeast

vegetable oil, for greasing and frying

METHOD: Put the milk and sugar in a saucepan and warm gently over a low heat until the sugar has dissolved; the milk should be just warm to the touch, but not hot. Remove from the heat and pour into a jug.

Sift the flour and salt into a large bowl and make a well in the centre. Add the yeast then pour the milk into the well. Whisk the milk into the flour until you have a smooth, thick batter. Cover the bowl with a clean tea towel and leave to stand in a warm place for 1 hour.

Heat a little oil in a large non-stick frying pan and grease 10 cm (4 inch) cooking rings with a little oil. Set the rings in the pan on a low heat, and pour a heaped tablespoon of the batter into each – you will probably need to do this in batches, depending on the size of your pan. Cook for 3–4 minutes until tiny bubbles appear on the surface of the crumpets. When the bubbles start to burst, turn the crumpets over and cook for a further minute. Remove from the pan and keep warm. Repeat with the remaining batter then serve warm with butter and jam.

TIP: Cook the crumpets on the lowest heat possible: you'll get more air bubbles, resulting in lighter crumpets.

№ 11

TOASTED TEACAKES

✳

Sometimes you can't decide between wanting something sweet or savoury with your tea, and I think the humble teacake bridges the gap! Perfect with lashings of salted butter on a rainy day. They also make a great breakfast alternative when rushing out the door.

MAKES 8

300 ml (½ pint) lukewarm water

50 g (2 oz) butter, softened

10 g (½ oz) fast-action dried yeast

60 g (2½ oz) caster sugar

500 g (1 lb 2 oz) strong white flour

10 g (½ oz) salt

50 g (2 oz) currants

50 g (2 oz) raisins

finely grated zest of 1 orange

beaten egg, for glazing

METHOD: Mix together the water and butter then add the yeast and half the sugar.

In a free-standing mixer, mix the flour, salt and the remaining sugar. Add the yeast mixture and mix with a dough hook for about 3 minutes on the lowest setting and then 6 minutes on the next one up.

Transfer the dough to a large oiled bowl and put in a warm place for at least 1 hour until it has doubled in size.

Add the dried fruit and orange zest to the dough and knead in until it is all incorporated. Divide the dough into 8 pieces and then shape into balls. The easiest way to ensure you get an even shape and surface is to throw each ball of dough on to your work surface and then use your hand to gently shape it, turning the ball of dough in small quarter-turns as you do so. Place on a baking sheet with plenty of space between them. Glaze with beaten egg and leave for another hour.

Preheat the oven to 200°C (400°F), gas mark 6, and bake for about 10–15 minutes until well-risen and golden brown all over.

TIP: You don't have to use currants and raisins – try dried cherries for a change!

'A pot of Earl Grey
and a big china cup
and the world seems a
happier place.'

LISA

№ 12

EARL GREY

TEA LOAF

My great-grandma always made tea loaf, a great old-fashioned staple at the table. I love it with butter and it's also great as a quick breakfast if you're running out of the door! The recipe says soak the fruit overnight and really you should for the best flavour, but I have made this on the same day (not being the most patient person) and as long as you soak the fruit for at least a few hours it'll be fine!

MAKES 1 LARGE LOAF

225 g (8 oz) raisins

225 g (8 oz) sultanas

125 g (4½ oz) dried figs, chopped

125 g (4½ oz) glacé cherries, halved

110 g (4 oz) chopped dried apricots

1 Earl Grey tea bag

110 g (4 oz) light muscovado sugar

110 g (4 oz) dark muscovado sugar

juice and zest of 1 orange

butter, for greasing

110 g (4 oz) ground almonds

1 tablespoon golden syrup

2 eggs, beaten

450 g (1 lb) self-raising flour

1 teaspoon ground mixed spice

100 ml (3½ fl oz) whole milk

METHOD: Combine the fruits in a large heatproof mixing bowl. Pour 300 ml (10 fl oz) boiling water onto the tea bag and leave to brew for a minute or so. Discard the tea bag then dissolve the sugars in the hot tea, add the orange juice and zest, and pour over the fruit. Stir to combine, then cover and leave to soak overnight.

The next day preheat the oven to 150°C (300°F), gas mark 2, and grease and line a 900 g (2 lb) loaf tin with greaseproof paper.

Stir the ground almonds, golden syrup and beaten eggs into the soaked fruit mixture then sift in the flour and mixed spice. Stir to combine, adding the milk if the mixture seems a little stiff, then spoon into the lined tin. Bake for 2–2¼ hours, or until a skewer inserted into the middle comes out clean. Transfer to a wire rack and leave to cool completely. Cut into thick slices and serve spread with butter.

№ 13

RHUBARB

FANTASY LOAF

✳

The recipe for fantasy cake in my first book, *Recipes from my Mother for my Daughter*, is probably one of the most popular and many of my lovely Twitter followers tweet me about it. People have tried lots of variations on my original recipe and I make it with all sorts of fruit, but I've recently found that it works particularly well with rhubarb and as a loaf. A loaf helps keeps it lovely and moist – and they're easier to transport too. I like to wrap the loaf in cellophane and tie it with a pretty ribbon. It really is a foolproof recipe, and as it's not a light cake anybody new to baking doesn't have to worry about overbeating!

MAKES 1 LOAF

400 g (14 oz) pink rhubarb, cut into
   3 cm (1¼ inch) lengths
200 g (7 oz) caster sugar
175 g (6 oz) unsalted butter, softened,
   plus extra for greasing
150 g (5 oz) self-raising flour

2 eggs
3 tablespoons milk
100 g (3½ oz) ground almonds
1 teaspoon almond extract
icing sugar, for dusting

METHOD: Preheat the oven to 170°C (325°F), gas mark 3. Toss the rhubarb pieces in 50 g (2 oz) of the sugar then spread out in an even layer on a non-stick baking sheet. Roast for 10–12 minutes until just softened, then set aside to cool.

Grease a 900 g (2 lb) loaf tin and line with greaseproof paper.

Beat together the butter and remaining sugar, then sift in the flour and add the eggs, milk, almonds and almond extract. Fold through the cooled rhubarb.

Pour the mixture into the loaf tin and bake for 1–1¼ hours. Test with a skewer inserted into the centre – if it comes out clean, the cake is ready. Be careful not to overcook!

Cool on a wire rack and dust with icing sugar. The cake is best served just as it is cooling from warm to room temperature.

№ 14

SOUR CHERRY
& PISTACHIO STOLLEN

❋

I love stollen dough, but I'm not always so keen on the raisins. So I sat down with my lovely friend and brilliant home economist, Super Rich, and we created a raisin-free stollen! The sour cherries are super-sharp against the sweetness of the marzipan.

MAKES 1 LOAF

175 ml (6 fl oz) milk

75 g (3 oz) caster sugar

75 g (3 oz) salted butter, plus extra
for greasing

1 large egg

350 g (12 oz) strong white bread
flour, plus extra for dusting

2 x 7 g (¼ oz) sachets fast-action
dried yeast

100 g (3½ oz) sour cherries

100 g (3½ oz) glacé cherries, halved

100 g (3½ oz) shelled pistachios

200 g (7 oz) marzipan

2 tablespoons icing sugar, plus extra
for sprinkling

METHOD: Warm the milk, sugar and butter together gently in a saucepan over a low heat until the sugar has dissolved and the butter has melted; the milk should be just warm to the touch. Remove from the heat and pour into a jug. Whisk in the egg and set aside.

Sift the flour into a large bowl, make a well in the centre and add the yeast. Pour in the milk mixture and stir with a fork to form a rough dough. Turn out onto a clean surface and knead for 7–8 minutes until smooth and elastic. Work in the cherries and pistachios and knead for a further 2 minutes. Transfer to a clean bowl, cover with a tea towel and leave in a warm place for 1 hour.

Turn out the dough on to a lightly floured surface and pat into a rough rectangle, 20 x 25 cm (8 x 10 inches). Roll the marzipan into a sausage shape and lay down the middle of the dough. Fold the dough over the marzipan and pinch to seal. Lightly grease a non-stick baking tray with butter and lay the loaf on it, seam side down. Cover with a clean tea towel and leave in a warm place for 45 minutes. Preheat the oven to 180°C (350°F), gas mark 4. Bake in the preheated oven for 10 minutes then reduce the temperature to 150°C (300°F), gas mark 2, and bake for a further 30–40 minutes until golden brown. Transfer to a wire rack and leave to cool. Mix the icing sugar with a little water and brush over the stollen. Sprinkle with more icing sugar.

№ 15

CHOCOLATE CHIP HOT CROSS BUNS

✖

In ye olden days when I was a child, Easter seemed to be a lot more religious than it is today. On Good Friday most of the shops shut, or were open only in the morning, and I remember my wonderful granddad Lely cycling over with warm hot cross buns from the baker's. I loved how sour the little currants were and the pretty cross on top, and since that day I have always wanted to make my own but with chocolate chips, so here they are.

MAKES 12

200 ml (7 fl oz) milk

100 g (3½ oz) unsalted butter

zest of 1 orange

20 g (¾ oz) fresh yeast

50 g (2 oz) golden caster sugar

450 g (1 lb) strong white bread flour

½ teaspoon salt

2 eggs, beaten

150 g (5 oz) dark chocolate chips

FOR THE CROSSES

3 tablespoons plain flour

pinch of salt

FOR THE GLAZE

50 g (2 oz) caster sugar

METHOD: Pour the milk, butter and orange zest into a saucepan and bring to a simmer. Remove from the heat and leave to cool to room temperature. Whisk in the yeast and half of the sugar and set aside.

Put the remaining sugar, flour and salt into the bowl of a free-standing mixer fitted with a dough hook then pour in the milk and yeast mixture and the eggs. Knead for 3 minutes on a low speed, then turn the speed up to the next highest setting and knead for a further 6 minutes.

Tip the dough into a large bowl and cover with a clean tea towel. Leave in a warm place to rise for 1½ hours until doubled in size.

Turn the dough out on to a lightly floured work surface and flatten into a large rectangle. Scatter the chocolate chips over the dough then fold everything into the centre and knead for a couple of minutes until the chocolate is evenly distributed through the dough.

Continued overleaf

✳

Divide the dough into 12 equal pieces and roll each into a smooth ball. The easiest way to ensure you get an even shape and surface is to throw each ball of dough onto your work surface and then use your hand to gently shape it, turning the ball of dough in small quarter-turns as you do so. Place the buns on two baking sheets lined with greaseproof paper, leaving a little space in between each one. The dough will rise and they will then join together in the oven.

Cover the trays with a clean tea towel and leave to rise for 1 hour until the dough has doubled in size. Preheat the oven to 200°C (400°F), gas mark 6.

For the crosses, mix the flour and salt with enough cold water to make a stiff paste then spoon into a piping bag fitted with a 3 mm (⅛ inch) plain nozzle. Pipe a cross on to each bun and bake for 18–20 minutes until golden brown.

While the buns are baking, pour the sugar into a small saucepan with 50 ml (2 fl oz) water and bring to the boil. Boil for 3–4 minutes until syrupy then remove from the heat. Once the buns are cooked, brush with the glaze while still warm then leave to cool completely.

№ 16

ICED BUNS

✤

This is a recipe from the lovely Mr Paul Hollywood. I was making iced buns using a different recipe and one day I decided to try out his – it was fantastic, the easiest to follow, and I got beautiful light iced buns. Paul is a lovely man as well as a brilliant baker and I feel very lucky to know him.

MAKES 14

40 g (1½ oz) butter, plus extra for greasing

50 g (2 oz) caster sugar

150 ml (5 fl oz) milk

140 ml (4½ fl oz) water

2 x 7 g (¼ oz) sachets fast-action dried yeast

500 g (1 lb 2 oz) strong white flour

2 teaspoons salt

2 eggs

FOR THE GLAZE AND DECORATION

200 g (7 oz) icing sugar

5 tablespoons water

7 glacé cherries, halved

METHOD: Preheat the oven to 220°C (425°F), gas mark 7, and grease a baking tray.

Heat the butter, sugar, milk and water in a saucepan until the mixture reaches blood temperature (38°C/100°F). Stir in the yeast.

Tip the flour and salt into the bowl of a freestanding mixer fitted with a dough hook and add the milk mixture and the eggs. Mix for about 4 minutes on a low speed then increase the speed and mix for a further 6 minutes.

Turn the dough out on to a floured work surface and knead a little more. Put the dough in a clean bowl, cover with a damp cloth and leave in a warm place for 1 hour.

Divide the dough into 14 pieces and shape into round buns. Place on the prepared baking tray, spaced apart as they will double in size. Return to a warm place for about 45 minutes.

Bake in the preheated oven for about 7 minutes then leave to cool. They should be light and fluffy, not too golden.

Meanwhile, mix the icing sugar and water together – it needs to be quite thick and sticky. Dip the cooled buns into the icing and then place half a glacé cherry on top. Yum!

№ 17

JAM DOUGHNUTS

✖

This is a lovely recipe from my friend John Whaite. These doughnuts really are the best I have ever tasted. When we made them for the photo shoot Billie ate three in one sitting! Pack them with jam so when you bite into them it dribbles down your chin, and try not licking your lips until you've eaten the whole doughnut!

MAKES 10

500 g (1 lb 2 oz) strong white flour

10 g (½ oz) salt

50 g (2 oz) caster sugar

1 x 7 g (¼ oz) sachet fast-action
   dried yeast

240 ml (8½ fl oz) milk

40 g (1½ oz) unsalted butter

2 eggs

FOR THE FILLING AND COATING

375 g (13 oz) any homemade jam
   from pages 196–197 or
   good-quality bought jam

caster sugar, for dusting

FOR DEEP-FRYING

3 litres (5¼ pints) sunflower oil

METHOD: First make a simple, enriched bread dough. Put the flour in a large mixing bowl, stir in the salt and sugar, then add the yeast.

Put the milk and butter in a saucepan over a medium heat and warm until you can just hold your finger in the milk without needing to snatch it back quickly. Mix well so that the butter melts, then add the eggs and beat them in.

Slowly add the liquid ingredients to the dry ingredients, mixing them together with a dough scraper or wooden spoon. When the liquid has been incorporated, tip the contents of the bowl out on to the worktop and knead for 10 minutes. The mixture will be extremely sticky, so the best way to knead it is by picking it up and slamming it on to the counter top, then folding it over. (This is why a dough scraper is a great tool.) If you have a freestanding electric mixer fitted with a dough hook, it might be easier to use it to knead the dough for 5 minutes on low.

When the dough is smooth and elastic, place it in a floured bowl and cover with a damp cloth. Leave to rise for 1 hour.

Continued overleaf

After the dough has risen, weigh it into 10 equal pieces (around 86 g/3¼ oz each). Roll these pieces into perfect balls and place on a floured baking sheet or board, spaced well apart. Cover with greased cling film and leave to rise again for 45 minutes.

Meanwhile, put the jam in a saucepan and heat just until it is runny. Sieve the jam into a bowl to remove any bits.

Pour the caster sugar on to a plate and place next to a wire rack. Pour the sunflower oil into a deep-fat fryer or large saucepan, making sure you don't fill your pan more than just under half full of oil.

Fifteen minutes before the dough balls are ready, heat the deep-fat fryer to 170°C (325°F). If you don't have a kitchen thermometer, test the heat of the oil by dropping a cube of bread into it: if it sizzles, the oil is ready. Fry the doughnuts two or three at a time, for about 3–4 minutes each side. Remove from the fryer using a slotted spoon and drain on kitchen paper for a minute, then dip in the sugar to coat well and place on the wire rack.

Put the jam into a pastry syringe, a plastic squeezy bottle with a nozzle, or a piping bag with a small plain nozzle. Make a small incision in the side of each doughnut using a sharp knife, then inject each one with a little jam, aiming to get it right into the centre. If jam starts to ooze out, simply dip the hole into the caster sugar and stand the doughnut up so the hole is on top. Devour.

NOTE:
You can also use custard from the trifle recipe on page 192.

№ 18

Croissant & Apricot Bread & Butter Pudding

When people come to stay, as well as making muffins and cowboy breakfasts, I seem to buy a load of croissants! The thing is, they don't all get eaten and they don't last, so this is an ideal way to use up the leftovers.

SERVES 6

- 25 g (1 oz) lightly salted butter
- 400 ml (14 fl oz) milk
- 200 ml (7 fl oz) double cream
- 1 vanilla pod, seeds scraped out, or 1 teaspoon vanilla extract
- 50 g (2 oz) caster sugar
- 3 large eggs plus 3 egg yolks
- 125 g (4½ oz) apricot jam
- 6 x day-old croissants, cut into 15 mm (⅝ inch) thick slices
- 100 g (3½ oz) chopped dried apricots

METHOD: Preheat the oven to 170°C (325°F), gas mark 3. Generously grease the base and sides of a 2.5 litre (4½ pint) ovenproof dish with the butter and set aside. Combine the milk, cream and vanilla pod and seeds (or extract) in a saucepan and bring to just simmering point.

Meanwhile whisk the sugar, eggs and egg yolks in a large bowl. Pour the hot milk mixture over the eggs and sugar and whisk to combine. Discard the vanilla pod.

Mix the apricot jam with 2 tablespoons of hot water to loosen then spread over the slices of croissant. Arrange the croissant slices in overlapping layers on the bottom of the dish, sprinkling the chopped apricots between the layers.

Pour the custard mixture over the top and leave to soak for 15–20 minutes. Bake in the preheated oven for 35–40 minutes until golden brown. Leave to stand for 10 minutes before serving.

№ 19

TRADITIONAL TRIFLE

✳

There's something about trifle that conjures up memories of my great-aunt Elsie's house. I don't have many memories of Auntie Elsie's food. Whether it was because she didn't really cook or was too old I don't know, but I do remember her making trifle and me going to her larder (I can smell it now as I type) and getting those sugared jelly diamonds and eating them along with glacé cherries. So this is in your honour, Auntie!

SERVES 8–10

FOR THE BASE

135 g (4¾ oz) raspberry or
   strawberry jelly

8 trifle sponges (or I like to use slices
   of Madeira cake)

1 x 410 g (14½ oz) tin peach slices

400 g (14 oz) frozen strawberries
   and raspberries

FOR THE CUSTARD

500 ml (18 fl oz) whole milk

1 vanilla pod, split and seeds
   scraped out

5 egg yolks

30 g (1 oz) caster sugar

2 teaspoons cornflour

TO FINISH AND DECORATE

250 ml (9 fl oz) double cream

glacé cherries and jelly diamonds

30 g (1 oz) toasted flaked almonds

METHOD: Make up the jelly following the packet instructions and allow it to cool until just starting to set. Cover the base of a large glass bowl (mine is about 25 cm/10 inches wide) with a layer of trifle sponges or sponge-cake strips then place a layer of drained fruit on top. Pour over the semi-liquid jelly so that it soaks the sponge and just submerges the fruit. Place the bowl in the fridge until the jelly has set completely.

While the jelly is setting, make the custard. Pour the milk and vanilla pod and seeds into a saucepan and bring to a simmer. Meanwhile, whisk together the egg yolks, sugar and cornflour in a large heatproof bowl. Pour the milk through a sieve on to the egg yolk mixture and whisk to combine.

Return the mixture to a clean heavy-based pan and set over a low heat. Cook gently for 2–3 minutes, stirring constantly, until the custard is thick enough to coat the back of a spoon. As soon as the custard is cooked, pour into a serving jug – this will prevent the residual

heat from the pan overcooking the custard. Set aside to cool.

When the jelly has set, remove the trifle from the fridge and add a layer of cooled custard about 3 cm (1¼ inches) thick. If your bowl is deep enough you can repeat the layers to make a double-decker trifle.

Whip the cream until it is stiff and standing in peaks, and spread or pipe evenly over the top of the trifle. Finally, decorate with glacé cherries, jelly diamonds and flaked almonds.

№ 20

LEMON CURD TARTLETS

These are delicious mouthfuls of lemony loveliness, especially if you've made the lemon curd yourself (see my grandma's recipe overleaf). You don't have to use lemon curd, of course; you can use whatever jam you like! I have included a couple of my favourite jam recipes here.

MAKES 36

FOR THE SHORTCRUST PASTRY

375 g (13 oz) plain flour

175 g (6 oz) cold butter, cubed, plus extra for greasing

pinch of salt

1–2 tablespoons cold water

FOR THE FILLING

420 g (15 oz) jar of lemon curd (or make your own!)

METHOD: To make the pastry, put the flour, butter, and salt in a food processor or stand mixer and pulse until the mixture resembles fine breadcrumbs. Add the cold water and pulse again until a dough starts to form. Shape into a flattish ball, wrap in cling film and chill for 30 minutes.

Preheat the oven to 190°C (375°F), gas mark 5, and grease three 12-hole mini tartlet/canapé tins with a little butter. Roll out the pastry to the thickness of a pound coin then cut out 36 discs of pastry; the pastry discs should be slightly wider than the holes in the tins.

Line the tins with the pastry discs, prick the bottoms with a fork and transfer to the freezer for 20 minutes until firm. Line each pastry case with a little square of baking paper and fill with baking beans, or roll pieces of tin foil into balls and place them in the pastry cases. Bake the little pastry cases for about 10 minutes until lightly golden.

Fill each pastry case with 1 teaspoon of lemon curd and return to the oven for 5 minutes. Transfer to a wire rack to cool.

TIP: This is a great basic pastry for pretty much anything, sweet or savoury.

BETTY'S LEMON CURD

This recipe is from my grandma Betty's well-thumbed recipe book. The pages are all falling out but there's nothing like using a recipe written in my grandma's beautiful handwriting. I love the sharpness of this curd.

MAKES 1 X 420 G (15 OZ) JAR

225 g (8 oz) caster sugar

60 g (2½ oz) unsalted butter

zest of 1 unwaxed lemon

juice of 2 lemons

2 large eggs, beaten

METHOD: Put the sugar, butter, lemon zest and juice into a non-stick pan and place over a low heat. Stir gently with a whisk until the butter has melted then whisk in the beaten eggs; you'll see it start to thicken. Switch to a wooden spoon and stir gently for 10–15 minutes. It should thicken enough to cling to the back of the spoon. Remove from the heat and leave to cool, stirring occasionally. When cool, pour into a sterilised jar.

STRAWBERRY & VANILLA JAM

For me, the addition of vanilla makes this easy strawberry jam all the more delicious.

MAKES ABOUT 2 KG (4½ LB)

1.5 kg (3 lb 5 oz) strawberries

1.5 kg (3 lb 5 oz) jam sugar

juice of 2 lemons

1–2 vanilla pods, seeds scraped out

METHOD: Before starting, put two or three saucers in the freezer ready for later. Put all the ingredients, including the vanilla pods, into a preserving pan and heat very slowly so that the sugar dissolves and doesn't burn.

Bring to the boil once the sugar has dissolved and simmer for about 5 minutes or so until the jam reaches setting point. To test if the jam has set, drop a teaspoonful onto one of the cold saucers; if it forms a skin that wrinkles when pushed, the jam is ready. If the jam isn't quite set, bring it back to the boil and cook for another 3–4 minutes, or until it reaches setting point.

Leave to cool for a good 15 minutes then discard the vanilla pods and spoon into sterilised jars. Leave to cool completely before sealing.

CHERRY JAM

I get real satisfaction out of making jam; I like the whole process, from sterilising the jars to the stirring and skimming! A tip here is to let the mixture cool quite a bit before putting it into jars and to keep stirring it in the jars so that the cherries don't sink to the bottom.

MAKES ABOUT 2 KG (4½ LB)

1 kg (2 lb 4 oz) fresh cherries, pitted

1 teaspoon almond extract

1 kg (2 lb 4 oz) jam sugar

juice of 2 lemons

250 ml (9 fl oz) pectin

METHOD: Before starting, put two or three saucers in the freezer ready for later. Put the cherries and almond extract into a large preserving pan with 150 ml (5 fl oz) water, bring to the boil and cook for 10 minutes until the cherries have softened. Add the sugar and lemon juice and stir until the sugar has dissolved completely.

Add the pectin, stir again and bring back to the boil. Cook for a further 8–10 minutes, skimming any scum that forms on the surface. To test if the jam has set, drop a teaspoonful onto one of the cold saucers; if it forms a skin that wrinkles when pushed, the jam is ready. If the jam isn't quite set, bring it back to the boil and cook for another 3–4 minutes or until it reaches setting point. Divide the jam between sterilised jars and leave to cool completely before sealing.

№ 21

RASPBERRY RIPPLE
ICE CREAM SANDWICHES

✖

I love those ice cream sandwiches you get on holiday, where the biscuit is a bit soft next to the ice cream. They remind me of late afternoons on the beach, when the sun is still high but people start leaving and the beach becomes quieter, and you sit and have your ice cream and wish your holiday would never end! Also there's something about the smell of cooked raspberries that transports your kitchen to the height of summer...

SERVES 16–20

200 ml (7 fl oz) whole milk

150 ml (5 fl oz) double cream

1 vanilla pod, split and seeds
  scraped out

3 large egg yolks

75 g (3 oz) caster sugar

FOR THE RASPBERRY RIPPLE

250 g (9 oz) raspberries

50 g (2 oz) caster sugar

TO SERVE

Rich Tea biscuits

METHOD: Pour the milk, cream, vanilla pod and seeds into a saucepan and bring to a simmer. Whisk the egg yolks and sugar together in a large heatproof bowl, then strain the milk and cream through a sieve on to the mixture. Stir to combine then pour into a clean heavy-based pan and set over a low heat. Cook gently for 2–3 minutes, stirring constantly, until the custard is thick enough to coat the back of a spoon.

As soon as the custard is cooked, pour into a serving jug; this will prevent the residual heat of the pan from overcooking the custard. Press a piece of cling film on to the surface of the custard (to prevent a skin from forming) and chill for 2–3 hours, or overnight.

Meanwhile, make the raspberry ripple. Put the raspberries in a saucepan with the sugar, bring to the boil and cook for 2–3 minutes until the raspberries start to collapse. Remove from the heat, leave to cool slightly then return to the heat and boil for 2 minutes. Pass the mixture through a fine sieve (if you want to remove the seeds), transfer to a bowl and cover with cling film. Transfer to the fridge to cool.

TIP: If you don't want to make this many sandwiches in one go you can, of course, freeze the rest of the ice cream and use it for cones or serve with puddings.

Put a large bowl or container in the freezer. Pour the vanilla custard into an ice-cream machine and churn until just set. Spoon into the frozen bowl, add the cooled raspberry syrup and fold through to create a rippled effect. Spoon into a large plastic container, cover with a lid and freeze for 3–4 hours until firm.

Take the ice cream out of the freezer 30 minutes before serving and leave it to soften at room temperature. Sandwich scoops of ice cream between two Rich Tea biscuits and serve.

№ 22

RASPBERRY
CHAMPAGNE JELLIES

✗

I think that we are all still big kids at heart, and you can't really beat jelly and ice cream…
unless, of course, there's champagne in it too! When you pour in the jelly, you do it in
layers so that the fruit doesn't float to the top – I love how the bubbles in the champagne
create stripes in the jelly!

SERVES 4–6

400 g (14 oz) raspberries

50 g (2 oz) caster sugar

8 gelatine leaves

500 ml (18 fl oz) chilled champagne,
prosecco or sparkling wine

METHOD: Set aside the 12 best-looking raspberries and put the remainder in a pan with the
sugar and 2 tablespoons of water. Bring to the boil then simmer for 3–4 minutes until the
raspberries start to break down. Pour into a muslin jelly bag and leave to hang over a jug
for 3–4 hours; do not squeeze the bag as this will result in a cloudy jelly.

Soak the gelatine leaves in cold water for about 5 minutes. Pour the raspberry juice into a
saucepan and heat gently. Once warm, remove the juice from the heat. Squeeze the excess
water from the gelatine leaves and stir them into the warm raspberry juice.

Pour the liquid into a measuring jug and top up to 800 ml (1½ pints) with the chilled
champagne. Half-fill 4 or 6 serving glasses and transfer to the fridge for 2 hours or until just
set. Place 3 raspberries on top of each jelly then top up with the remaining jelly mixture.
Return to the fridge for a further 2 hours until set.

№ 23

CUCUMBER & MINT WATER

✖

Last year I spent five days on the idyllic Greek island of Mykonos. It was just at the beginning of the season, and the weather was beautiful and the island pretty quiet. We ate gorgeous food and lazed about in the sun. Every day the waiter would make different waters for us to try. These were my favourites and I had to include them. Perfectly refreshing!

MAKES 1.8 LITRES (3 PINTS)

1 cucumber

1 sprig of fresh mint

1.8 litres (3 pints) water

lots of ice

METHOD: Peel the cucumber lengthways with a vegetable peeler until you get to the seeds. Put the skin and flesh in a jug and add the mint, water and ice. Give it a good stir.

Leave in the fridge to infuse for 1 hour.

This refreshing drink will keep in the fridge for 2 days.

GINGER & LEMON WATER

MAKES 1.8 LITRES (3 PINTS)

3–4 slices fresh root ginger

1 lemon, sliced

1 teaspoon grated lemon zest

1.8 litres (3 pints) water

METHOD: Add the ginger, lemon slices and lemon zest to the water.

Leave to stand in the fridge overnight. Strain and serve.

Be sure to keep refrigerated and drink within 2 days.

№ 24

LEMON ICED TEA

✳

This being tea, it is THE summer drink for me! We seem to have come around to the idea of iced coffee in this country, but iced tea is still thin on the ground and I don't know why! Such a simple drink to make and so refreshing; for the nation of tea lovers that we are, this one is for you!

MAKES 1.8 LITRES (3 PINTS)

3 Earl Grey tea bags
1.8 litres (3 pints) water
sugar, to taste

1 lemon, sliced
lots of ice

METHOD: Place the teabags in a jug. Boil 600 ml (1 pint) of the water and pour over the tea bags. Leave to infuse for 3–5 minutes – no longer than this or the tea will taste bitter.

Add a couple of teaspoons of sugar and stir.

Add the lemon slices and 600 ml (1 pint) cold water. Taste the tea and add more sugar if necessary.

Add the remaining 600 ml (1 pint) cold water and lots of ice. Refrigerate before serving.

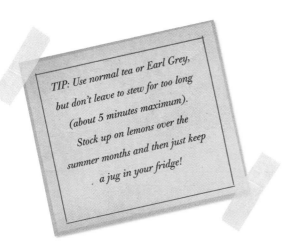

TIP: Use normal tea or Earl Grey, but don't leave to stew for too long (about 5 minutes maximum). Stock up on lemons over the summer months and then just keep a jug in your fridge!

№ 25

RICH'S ROSEMARY G&TEA

To celebrate my obsessive love of tea, I wanted to include a fun cocktail. My super-talented home economist friend Rich and I came up with this sharp, frothy, boozy tea! Really refreshing on long, hot summer days.

SERVES 2

FOR THE EARL GREY SYRUP

100 g (3½ oz) caster sugar

2 tablespoons loose-leaf Earl Grey tea

FOR THE COCKTAIL

50 ml (2 fl oz) gin

juice of ½ lemon

2 sprigs fresh rosemary, plus extra for garnish

25 ml (1 fl oz) Earl Grey syrup

1 medium egg white

ice

soda water

METHOD: For the syrup, pour the sugar into a saucepan with 100 ml (3½ fl oz) water, bring to the boil and simmer for 2 minutes until the sugar has completely dissolved. Add the tea, stir and leave to steep for 5 minutes. Strain and leave to cool completely.

To make the cocktail, combine all of the ingredients apart from the soda water in a shaker and top up with ice.

Shake hard for 1 minute until the outside of the shaker begins to frost.

Strain into a highball glass with a couple of large ice cubes and top up with soda water. Garnish with a sprig of rosemary and serve.

LET'S PICNIC!

Tarts were traditionally made to show off all the lovely produce you had grown in your garden – they were so pretty that your eyes ate them before your mouth did! Pies did almost the opposite and were hearty ways to use up everything you had in your larder. This chapter is full of the prettiest tarts to lay out on your best tablecloth as well comforting sweet pies to serve with jugs of custard, and mini mouthfuls to take on picnics or snack on whenever you fancy. ❦

№ 1

PEAR & FRANGIPANE TART

A slice of this tart with a cup of tea is a beautiful thing, but served warm with a spoon of mascarpone or crème fraîche and you have a majestic dinner party dessert!

SERVES 8

1 quantity sweet shortcrust pastry (see page 216)
4 pears
1 lemon
1 orange
225 g (8 oz) caster sugar
1 vanilla pod
575 ml (1 pint) white wine
575 ml (1 pint) water

FOR THE FRANGIPANE

115 g (4 oz) butter, softened, at room temperature
115 g (4 oz) caster sugar
2 eggs, beaten
115 g (4 oz) ground almonds
1 tablespoon plain flour
1 tablespoon flaked almonds, to serve

METHOD: Roll out the pastry on to a lightly floured surface to a thickness of about a pound coin and use it to line a 25 cm (10 inch) deep tart tin. Allow the pastry to hang over the edge, but push it down into the base and up the side. Prick the base with a fork and transfer to the fridge for 30 minutes to firm up. Preheat the oven to 190°C (375°F), gas mark 5.

Scrunch up some greaseproof paper and place it on top of the pastry base. Fill it with baking beans and bake the tart for 15–20 minutes. Remove the paper and beans and return to the oven for 10 minutes or so, until the pastry is golden. Leave to cool while you prepare the pears. Use a serrated knife to trim off any excess pastry from around the edge.

Peel the pears, put them in a saucepan with all the other ingredients and bring to the boil. Reduce the heat, cover with a circle of greaseproof paper and poach for about 20 minutes, until the pears are cooked all the way through but not soft. Leave to cool in the cooking liquid. Preheat the oven to 150°C (300°F), gas mark 2.

To make the frangipane, beat together the butter and sugar. Beat the eggs into the mixture, adding a little at a time and interspersing with the almonds and flour. If you add the eggs all in one go the mixture may split. Spoon half the frangipane into the tart shell. Cut the pears in half and arrange on top. Spoon over the rest of the frangipane, smoothing to level, and sprinkle with the flaked almonds. Bake in the oven for 1 hour. Serve while still warm.

TIP: You can use tinned pears (or even peaches) for this. Just drain them – no need to poach them.

№ 2

NECTARINE & PISTACHIO
TART

I'm always keeping an eye out for quick and easy puddings. My friends and I have a lot of spur-of-the-moment dinner parties where everyone brings a dish and heads on over, so this is perfect for those occasions! This is great served with some crème fraîche on the side.

SERVES 8–10

butter, for greasing

1 quantity sweet shortcrust pastry
(see page 216)

50 g (2 oz) shelled pistachios,
chopped

150 g (5 oz) mascarpone or crème
fraîche

50 g (2 oz) ground almonds

zest of 1 orange

25 g (1 oz) caster sugar, plus extra for
sprinkling

3–4 nectarines, stoned and sliced

1 egg white, lightly whisked

METHOD: Preheat the oven to 180°C (350°F), gas mark 4.

Make the pastry following the method on page 216, adding the chopped pistachios at the last minute and reserving a few for the top of the tart. Rest in the fridge for 30 minutes.

Roll out the pastry on a lightly floured surface. Cut out a 24 cm (9½ inch) circle and place on a greased baking sheet.

Mix together the mascarpone or crème fraîche, almonds, orange zest and caster sugar. Spoon the cream on to the pastry, leaving a border of about 5 cm (2 inches) all the way round, and arrange the nectarine slices on top of the cream. Brush with the egg white, sprinkle with caster sugar and scatter over the reserved pistachios.

Bake in the preheated oven for about 30 minutes until the pastry is golden.

№ 3

BETTY'S BAKEWELL TART

✳

Another of my grandma Betty's recipes. I loved her Bakewell tart when I was growing up.
It was always a little rough around the edges but tasted wonderful!

SERVES 6–8

300 g (10 oz) raspberry jam

FOR THE SWEET SHORTCRUST PASTRY

250 g (9 oz) plain flour, plus extra for
    dusting

90 g (3¼ oz) caster sugar

175 g (6 oz) unsalted butter

zest of ¼ lemon

1 egg

FOR THE FILLING

175 g (6 oz) unsalted butter, at room
    temperature

175 g (6 oz) caster sugar

3 eggs, beaten

1 teaspoon almond extract

100 g (3½ oz) ground almonds

75 g (3 oz) semolina

METHOD: To make the pastry, tip the flour, sugar, butter and lemon zest into the bowl of
a food processor and pulse to form breadcrumbs. Add the egg and pulse again until the
pastry just comes together. Shape into a ball, flatten slightly and then chill in the fridge for
30 minutes.

Roll out the pastry onto a lightly floured surface to a thickness of about a pound coin and
use it to line a 23 cm (9 inch) loose-bottomed fluted tart tin. Allow the pastry to hang over
the edge, but push it down into the base and up the side. Prick the base with a fork and
transfer to the fridge for 30 minutes to firm up. Preheat the oven to 190°C (375°F), gas
mark 5.

Scrunch up some greaseproof paper and place it on top of the pastry base. Fill with baking
beans or rice and bake the tart for 15–20 minutes. Remove the paper and beans and return
to the oven for an extra 10 minutes, until the pastry is golden. Remove the pastry case from
the oven and leave to cool on a wire rack. Use a serrated knife to trim around the edge.

Cream the butter and sugar with an electric whisk until pale and fluffy then gradually beat in the eggs and almond extract. Fold in the ground almonds and semolina.

Spread the jam over the base of the pastry case then carefully spoon the frangipane mixture on top. Smooth the top with the back of a spoon then bake for 30 minutes until golden brown with a slight wobble in the centre. Transfer to a wire rack and leave to cool before turning out and slicing.

№ 4

CLAFOUTIS LIMOUSIN

✳

This is a great pudding, very easy and quick to whip up. Cherries soaked in brandy (stones removed!) are the best for this baked custard cake. Leave it to settle when it comes out of the oven and warn everyone that the cherries will be very hot. Serve with cream or ice cream and, if there's any left over after the first sitting, it's great cold the next day.

SERVES 4–6

400 ml (14 fl oz) milk

150 g (5 oz) flour

70 g (2¾ oz) caster sugar

pinch of salt

3 eggs

2 tablespoons rum (optional)

about 80 g (3 oz) butter, for greasing

200 g (7 oz) fresh cherries

icing sugar, for dusting

METHOD: Preheat the oven to 180°C (350°F), gas mark 4.

Put the milk in a saucepan and bring to the boil. Take off the heat and leave to cool.

To make the batter, mix the flour, sugar and salt together well, then beat in the eggs, one by one. With a spatula, incorporate the boiled milk very slowly and gently, *turning* the mixture rather than beating. Add the rum, if using.

Generously grease a 2 cm (¾ inch) deep, 25 cm (10 inch) diameter baking tin with butter and add the cherries, spreading them evenly. Pour the batter over the top and cook in the preheated oven for 30 minutes. Sprinkle with a little icing sugar before serving hot or cold.

NOTE: It may seem like a lot of butter, but you do need it all to stop the clafoutis from sticking to the tin.

№ 5

PANFORTE

※

John Torode made this for me at Christmas. It's perfect for making in huge batches and wrapping, first in rice paper and then with more decorative paper, to give as Christmas presents.

SERVES 8–10

30 g (1 oz) butter, plus extra for greasing

100 g (3½ oz) whole hazelnuts, coarsely chopped

100 g (3½ oz) blanched almonds

250 g (9 oz) mixed chopped candied peel

1 teaspoon grated lemon zest

70 g (2¾ oz) flour

½ teaspoon ground cinnamon

¼ teaspoon ground coriander

¼ teaspoon ground cloves

¼ teaspoon freshly grated nutmeg

pinch of white pepper

140 g (4½ oz) dried figs, coarsely chopped

100 g (3½ oz) caster sugar

60 g (2½ oz) runny honey

icing sugar, for dusting

METHOD: Preheat the oven to 180°C (350°F), gas mark 4, and line a loose-bottomed 23 cm (9 inch) cake tin with greased baking paper.

Spread the hazelnuts and almonds on a baking tray and roast them gently, turning regularly until they are golden. This will take about 8–10 minutes – they will turn from golden to burnt very quickly, so keep an eye on them. Remove from the oven and set aside to cool.

Reduce the oven temperature to 150°C (300°F), gas mark 2. In a large bowl, mix together the cooled nuts, mixed peel and lemon zest. Sift the flour and spices into another bowl.

Place the figs, sugar, honey and butter in a saucepan with a little splash of water and cook over a low heat for 5–10 minutes until the figs are lovely and sticky. Add this mixture to the nuts and mixed peel and stir well, then sift over the flour and spices and fold them into the mixture.

Spoon into the prepared tin and bake in the oven for 40–45 minutes until richly golden. Leave to cool in the tin for 5 minutes then turn out on to a wire rack to cool completely. Once cold, dust with icing sugar and serve or slice into wedges and wrap up to give as gifts. Wrapped and stored in an airtight container, panforte will keep for 6–8 months.

MINCE PIES
WITH FLAKY PASTRY

❋

I have always made my own mincemeat and mince pies. Usually I use basic shortcrust pastry for these (see page 216) but sometimes it's nice to mix it up a bit and flaky pastry works really well, too.

MAKES ABOUT 24

FOR THE FLAKY PASTRY
300 g (10½ oz) plain flour
200 g (7 oz) unsalted butter, chilled
    and cubed, plus extra for greasing
pinch of salt

1–2 tablespoons water
FOR THE FILLING
600 g (1¼ lb) mincemeat
    (see recipe overleaf)
icing sugar, for dusting (optional)

METHOD: Tip the flour, butter and salt into a food processor and pulse until you have a breadcrumb-like consistency. Add 1–2 tablespoons of water and pulse again until a dough is formed.

Shape the dough into a round, cover and rest in the fridge for 30 minutes.

Preheat the oven to 180°C (350°F), gas mark 4, and lightly grease two 12-hole bun tins.

When ready to use, roll the pastry out thinly, to about 5 mm (¼ inch), and use an 8 cm (3 inch) and a 7 cm (2¾ inch) cutter to cut 12 shapes of each size.

Place the bigger circles in the base of the tin, add a teaspoon of the mincemeat and cover with the smaller circles. Wet the rims with water to seal and prick the tops with a fork.

Bake in the preheated oven for 25–30 minutes. My grandma never glazed her pies, but you can brush them with egg yolk if you want them to be shiny. Dust with icing sugar if you like.

✖   BETTY'S MINCEMEAT   ✖

This recipe was in my first book, but it's such a classic that I have to include it here as well. Make loads and store it in jars in the fridge to use whenever the need for a mince pie strikes you! It will keep for ages. Grandma Betty's mincemeat recipe is really easy and you will feel very clever that you've made your own!

MAKES JUST OVER 2.5 KG (6 LB)

450 g (1 lb) currants

450 g (1 lb) shredded suet

450 g (1 lb) soft brown sugar

450 g (1 lb) sultanas

450 g (1 lb) raisins

450 g (1 lb) cooking apples (peeled weight)

1–2 tablespoons brandy

1 level teaspoon mixed spice

½ teaspoon cinnamon

METHOD: Preheat the oven to 170°C (325°F), gas mark 3, and put clean jars in to sterilise for at least 5 minutes.

Set aside the currants, suet and sugar then combine all the remaining ingredients in a food processor (or mince them with a sharp knife). Make sure the mixture still is a bit rough – don't make it too fine.

In a large bowl mix the currants, suet and sugar together with the processed ingredients.

Spoon into the prepared jars, leaving a 1 cm (½ inch) 'breathing space' at the top.

Cover with a waxed disc and a circle of cellophane, or a screw-top lid.

№ 7

NANA BEAN'S
COCONUT PIE

❧

This is a fabulous recipe from my friend Nige. He worked on the PR for my first two books and we became friends then. He's tried all my recipes and I love him for that! This is his recipe and his story…

'I have been visiting friends and family in Bermuda since I was a little boy. It is a tiny island in the middle of the Atlantic, with pink sand and is surrounded by coral reefs and turquoise ocean. Nana Bean cooks because she loves to, and if you are visiting the island she always sends care packages of her cakes and stews. They are all her own recipes and are all absolutely delicious. On my last visit, she made her coconut pie. It's light and rich and the coconut flavour reminds me of all the happy times I've spent on Bermuda.'

SERVES 6

FOR THE PASTRY

110 g (4 oz) vegetable shortening, plus extra for greasing

150 g (5 oz) plain flour

1 tablespoon sugar

1 teaspoon salt

2 tablespoons water

FOR THE FILLING

170 g (6 oz) desiccated coconut

3 eggs

400 g (14 oz) caster sugar

340 g (12 oz) evaporated milk

½ teaspoon vanilla extract

METHOD: Preheat the oven to 180°C (350°F), gas mark 4, and grease a 20 cm (8 inch) tart tin.

Make the pastry by pulsing the dry ingredients and vegetable shortening in a food processer and adding the water a tablespoon at a time until it comes together. Shape into a disc, cover in cling film and rest in the fridge for about 30 minutes.

Roll out the pastry to the thickness of a pound coin and line the tin with it. Do not trim off the excess pastry; leave it hanging over the edge. Bake in the oven for 20 minutes. Remove from the oven and then cut off the excess pastry from around the edge using a serrated knife. Leave to cool.

Make the filling by whisking all the ingredients together. Pour into the cooled pastry case and bake in the preheated oven for about 15–20 minutes, until the filling is set and the top is golden.

№ 8

APPLE & VANILLA CHARLOTTES

✳

There's something about an apple charlotte that immediately makes me feel cosy and warm, as if I've just been given a hug. On cold days, apple charlotte and custard after a great big family roast is just what the doctor ordered!

SERVES 6

100 g (3½ oz) unsalted butter, plus extra for greasing

6 Braeburn apples

50 g (2 oz) golden caster sugar

juice of ½ lemon

1 vanilla pod, seeds scraped out, or 1 tablespoon vanilla paste

12 thin slices day-old white bread, crusts removed

METHOD: Preheat the oven to 180°C (350°F), gas mark 4. Grease the insides of 6 dariole moulds or ramekins with plenty of butter and set aside.

Peel, core and cut the apples into small dice. Put into a saucepan with the sugar and lemon juice. Bring to the boil then simmer for 5 minutes until the apples are starting to soften. Remove from the heat and set aside to cool.

Melt the butter in a small saucepan and add the vanilla seeds or paste. Cut the slices of bread into fingers, place each in the melted butter and use to line the dariole moulds or ramekins, with the buttered side against the tin – do not trim the excess. Divide the apple filling between the ramekins and finish by folding over the excess bread fingers.

Put the moulds on to a baking tray and lay a sheet of greaseproof paper on top. Top with a second baking tray then bake for 25–30 minutes until golden brown. Leave to cool slightly before turning out on to serving plates. Serve with homemade custard (see page 233) or vanilla ice cream.

'Warm pie and a jug
of custard is like a
great big cuddle in a
bowl. Yum!!'

LISA

№ 9

DEEP-DISH APPLE PIE

✖

Apple pie… a favourite classic pud – but it's always nice to try out a slightly different recipe from the one you've been following for years! The neat layers make this particularly pretty to slice.

SERVES 6

2 x quantities of flaky pastry
   (see page 223)

2 large egg yolks, beaten

FOR THE FILLING

2.5 kg (5 lb 8 oz) Braeburn apples,
   peeled and cored

150 g (5 oz) demerara sugar,
   plus extra for dusting

1 teaspoon ground ginger

zest and juice of 1 lemon

1 tablespoon semolina

METHOD: Preheat the oven to 200°C (400°F), gas mark 6. Roll out half of the pastry to the thickness of a pound coin and use it to line a 23 cm (9 inch) deep-sided metal pie dish. Transfer to the freezer while you prepare the filling.

Slice the apples very thinly (use a mandolin if you have one) and toss with the sugar, ginger, lemon zest and juice. Remove the pastry case from the freezer, sprinkle the semolina over the base and pack the apple slices in tightly. Roll out the remaining pastry to form a lid. Brush the rim of the pastry base with a little beaten egg yolk, lay the lid on top and press down to seal. Pinch the edges of the pastry with your thumb, brush the top with egg yolk and make a small slit in the centre to allow steam to escape. Sprinkle with sugar. Return to the freezer for 20 minutes then bake the pie for 40–45 minutes, until golden brown and crisp. Leave to stand for 5 minutes before serving.

RHUBARB & CUSTARD POT PIES

❋

As I sit writing this the rain is streaming down my kitchen window and, although it's only three o'clock in the afternoon, it may as well be night-time – it's so dark! I have what is commonly known as the January blues, and all I want to do is sit in my pyjamas and Uggs with the fire on, watching films and cooking food that is going to make me feel better. These little pies will do just that…

SERVES 6

FOR THE RHUBARB

500 g (1 lb 2 oz) pink rhubarb,
    cut into 3 cm (1¼ inch) lengths

50 g (2 oz) caster sugar

zest and juice of 1 orange

1 vanilla pod, seeds scraped out

FOR THE CUSTARD

500 ml (18 fl oz) milk

1 vanilla pod, seeds scraped out

4 egg yolks

100 g (3½ oz) caster sugar

40 g (1½ oz) cornflour

FOR TOPPING THE PIES

1 quantity flaky pastry (see page 223)

2 egg yolks, beaten

caster sugar, to sprinkle

METHOD: Preheat the oven to 180°C (350°F), gas mark 4. Toss the rhubarb together with the sugar, orange zest and juice, and vanilla seeds. Tip into a roasting tray and bake for 10–12 minutes until just starting to soften. Remove the rhubarb from the tin with a slotted spoon then divide between 6 ramekins or small ovenproof dishes and leave to cool.

For the custard, pour the milk into a saucepan and add the vanilla pod and seeds. Bring to a gentle simmer. Tip the egg yolks, sugar and cornflour into a heatproof bowl and whisk together. Strain the hot milk through a fine sieve onto the egg-yolk mixture and whisk to combine. Return to the pan, bring to a simmer and cook for 5 minutes until thickened. Pour the custard over the rhubarb and set aside to cool.

Roll the pastry out to the thickness of a pound coin then cut out 6 discs the same diameter as the ramekins. Carefully lay the pastry discs on top of the custard and tuck the edges in neatly. Use a skewer to make 3–4 small holes in the pastry (to allow steam to escape) then brush each with beaten egg yolk and sprinkle with sugar. Bake for 20–25 minutes, until the pastry is golden brown and crisp. Leave to cool for 5–10 minutes before serving.

№ 11

HAM HOCK

& PEA PIES

✳

I love a raised pie… in fact, I love a pie, full-stop! These are great for any occasion, but they are especially good to take on a picnic – a delicious handful of crispy pastry surrounding ham, peas and jelly. Yum! You will need four 7.5 cm (3 inch) individual pork pie tins – approx. 280 ml (9 fl oz). See note overleaf.

MAKES 4 INDIVIDUAL PIES

FOR THE PASTRY

500 g (1 lb 2 oz) plain flour, plus
extra for dusting

1½ teaspoons salt

1 tablespoon icing sugar

200 g (7 oz) lard, chopped

200 ml (7 fl oz) water

FOR THE FILLING

350 g (12 oz) cooked ham hock,
shredded

2 bay leaves, shredded

small handful fresh flat-leaf parsley,
chopped, plus extra to garnish

few sprigs of fresh tarragon, chopped

100 g (3½ oz) frozen petit pois

salt and freshly ground black pepper

2 gelatine leaves

500 ml (18 fl oz) fresh chicken stock,
reduced down to 200 ml (7 fl oz)
over a medium heat

FOR THE GLAZE

2 egg yolks, beaten

METHOD: To make the pastry, sift the flour, salt and icing sugar into a large bowl. Combine the lard and water in a saucepan and heat gently until the lard has completely melted. Make a well in the centre of the flour then beat in the hot lard and water with a wooden spoon until you have a smooth dough. Turn out onto a clean surface and knead briefly until smooth. Set aside to cool a little, but you will need to use it while it is still warm and flexible, so don't leave it too long.

Preheat the oven to 200°C (400°F), gas mark 6.

Place the shredded ham hock in a large bowl with the herbs and peas. Mix well and season with a little salt and plenty of black pepper.

Continued overleaf

Roll out the pastry on a lightly floured surface so it is a little thicker than a pound coin and cut out 4 rough circles, each about 20 cm (8 inches) in diameter, making sure you save enough pastry to use as lids. Use the circles to line the 4 individual pork pie tins, pressing the pastry into each mould firmly so it fully lines the tin and comes up a little above the top rim.

Spoon the ham and pea mixture into the pastry and press down with the back of a spoon. Re-roll the trimmings and cut out 6 discs of pastry for the lids, each 8 cm (3 inches) in diameter. Brush with a little beaten egg yolk and press down on top of the filling to seal. Cut a small hole in the top of each pie and brush all over with egg yolk.

Place the tins on a baking tray and bake in the preheated oven for 40–45 minutes, until golden brown and crisp. Remove from the oven and carefully remove the pies from their moulds. Place the pies back on the baking tray and return to the oven for a further 10 minutes to make sure the sides are lovely and crisp. Then return the pies to their tins and transfer to a wire rack.

Meanwhile, soak the gelatine in cold water for a minute, then heat the reserved stock until steaming. Add the gelatine to the stock and stir to dissolve. Using a funnel, pour the stock into the holes in the top of the pies until each one is full – you may not need to use all the stock. Leave to cool. Once cool, transfer to the fridge for 2–3 hours or overnight if possible. Turn out of their tins and serve with piccalilli.

NOTE: Special pie tins are available from cookware shops and I think they make all the difference here. However, you can make smaller pies using an ordinary muffin tray. The amount of filling in this recipe is enough to make 11 smaller pies. Roll out the pastry and cut out 11 circles, each about 10 cm (4 inches) in diameter and use these to line the muffin cups. Fill each cup with the ham and pea mixture and then re-roll the pastry trimmings and cut out lids. Finish the recipe as above.

№ 12

MINI CORNISH PASTIES

If I couldn't live in London, the place I'd choose – in England anyway – is Cornwall. When I walk along the beaches there I can get a proper sense of perspective, which isn't always possible closer to home. Also, as soon as I get to Cornwall I want a pasty! There's nothing better than sitting on the beach at Marazion looking out at St Michael's Mount, eating a pasty and listening to the seagulls... rain or shine, I love this.

MAKES 8

1 quantity flaky pastry (see page 223)
2 egg yolks beaten with 2 teaspoons milk

FOR THE FILLING

175 g (6 oz) beef short rib (off the bone), finely diced
125 g (4½ oz) Charlotte potatoes, peeled and finely diced
90 g (3¼ oz) swede, peeled and finely diced
1 onion, peeled and finely diced
25 g (1 oz) unsalted butter, melted
splash of Worcestershire sauce
sea salt
freshly ground black pepper

METHOD: In a bowl, combine the ingredients for the filling, seasoning with salt and plenty of black pepper.

Dust a work surface with flour, roll out the pastry to the thickness of a pound coin and use a 10 cm (4 inch) cutter to cut out 8 discs.

Divide the filling between the pastry discs and brush around the edges with the egg wash. Bring the edges of the pastry up over the filling and pinch to seal. Crimp the edges and transfer to a baking sheet lined with greaseproof paper. Repeat with the remaining pastry and filling. Brush the pasties with egg wash then transfer to the fridge to chill for 1 hour until firm.

Preheat the oven to 180°C (350°F), gas mark 4.

Remove the pasties from the fridge and bake for 15 minutes. Turn the oven down to 150°C (300°F), gas mark 2, and bake for a further 25 minutes until golden brown.

№ 13

PORK & APPLE SAUSAGE ROLLS

A match made in heaven! Enough said…

MAKES 12

25 g (1 oz) butter, plus extra for greasing
2 shallots, finely chopped
1 garlic clove, finely chopped
1 apple, peeled and grated
2 sage leaves, finely chopped
400 g (14 oz) sausage meat
salt and freshly ground black pepper
375 g (13 oz) ready-rolled puff pastry
1 egg, beaten

METHOD: Preheat the oven to 180°C (350°F), gas mark 4, and grease a baking tray.

In a frying pan, melt the butter and sweat the shallots and garlic until translucent and softened. Add the grated apple and soften for a few minutes before adding the sage. Mix the shallot mixture with the sausage meat and season.

Cut the pastry sheet in half lengthways. Halve the sausage mixture and roll into two long sausage shapes and place them in the middle of the pastry rectangles.

Brush the edges of the pastry with the beaten egg and roll up. Cut each length into 6 sausage rolls.

Place on the baking tray, brush over with the egg and bake for 25–30 minutes, until golden, crisp and puffed. Leave to cool for 10 minutes before devouring.

TIP: The only thing that can improve these is a little bit of mustard (or ketchup!).

INGREDIENT NOTES

& KITCHEN TIPS

✕

A QUICK WORD ON INGREDIENTS AND EQUIPMENT

❋

My recipes are pretty flexible so play around with them and make them your own.
To help you on your way, here are a few notes on the ingredients and bits of
kit that I use most often.

INGREDIENTS

BUTTER: Generally, I use unsalted butter when I'm baking, but if you don't have any then salted is fine. I sometimes quite like the added salt, especially if I'm making something very sweet and chocolatey as it can give it a lovely savoury contrast.

EGGS: I use medium free-range eggs. When you're making cakes, the size of your eggs can make a difference to how well they rise. And I always keep them at room temperature.

FOOD COLOURING: I don't usually like to mention brands but Sugarflair food colouring really is the best. The colours stay really bright and won't make your baking murky or dull.

MILK: You can use whatever kind of milk you like – goat's milk is a great alternative if you can't eat dairy. I usually use semi-skimmed milk for baking, though.

SPRAY CAKE RELEASE: This is something I only came across recently, and I now use it in place of butter to grease everything!

KIT

MIXERS AND FOOD PROCESSORS: A food mixer will stand you in good stead and save you time in the kitchen, but you don't *have* to have one. All my recipes can be made the good old-fashioned way by hand!

OVENS: Every oven is different, and it can take a little while to get to know how yours behaves – some can be a little hotter, and some can cook unevenly. If I'm cooking something from a new recipe, I'll usually bake it for 5–10 minutes less than the method suggests and give it a quick test to see how much longer it needs.

PIPING BAGS: Piping bags have become my new best friends. When I can, I order the industrial blue ones from online catering sites, as they're very strong and good quality. If you don't have piping bags you can spoon your icing on, but I think they give a really professional finish and are really easy to use.

✖ INDEX ✖

D

E

F

G

THANK YOU!

✳

First of all thank you to my brilliant A Team! To Super Rich, the clue is the name and I love you, the brilliant Leonie, my amazing Lizzie Kamenetzky, and gorgeous Poppy. To Polly Webb-Wilson, who just gets it, gets me and is super stylist, and to Olivia. To Chris Terry, who I feel lucky enough to consider a friend as well as the best photographer in the land, and Danny, you make it all so much fun! To David Eldridge who has made every page of this book beautiful.

To my new BFF Laura Herring, thank you for helping me see it all so much more clearly and for helping me fall in love with my book. Can we just hang out?

To the wonderful team at Simon & Schuster, especially Ian and Suzanne for really listening.

To Justine for making me look presentable and talking clothes and food. I love you!

To my John, who makes everything possible and makes me believe, who listens and chats and understands me! I properly love you.

To my family, my daddy, my sister Victoria, I can't live without you. To Allen, Lola, Eva Rose, Jonny and especially my truly beautiful daughter, Billie, who inspires me every day.

To all the amazing people I get to work with, who have given me recipes and ideas and love: Ben Ebbrell, Rachel Allen, Natalie Coleman, Paul Hollywood, Mary Berry, Jo Wheatley, John Whaite, Nigel Stoneman, Steve Groves, Nikki Morgan, Katie Liasis, Helen Lowe (who is Myrtleberry Cakes), Julia Alger and Melissa from Simply Vintage Designs.

To Amy and the team at Taste PR.

Also thank you to my godmothers Ann, Pat and Nina and to aunt Sue for your recipes and support. To Angie and Nic for being my bezzers! And The Food Network for all your support.

To my agent Jonny McWilliams: you go above and beyond and are SO much more than just an agent, together we can conquer the world ;)

To everyone who supports me on Twitter and watches me on telly and buys my books or tries my recipes, thank you because you make it all possible.

And to my mummy and grandmother Betty, my Lely and my Nanna because you are always around me xxx